A HARD LIVING

A small Western Ocean schooner Little Secret lies on the tideline in Fowey - a port familiar to many yachtsmen.
National Maritime Museum.

A HARD LIVING

Westcountry seafarers
in Victorian England.

These factual reports are taken from the Western Daily Mercury,
the Western Morning News, and the West Briton newspapers.

Ian Gallacher.
Whistlestop.

First published in 1992 by
Whistlestop
Glebelands, Calstock,
Cornwall. PL18 9SG.

Copyright Ian Gallacher 1992. All rights reserved.

Overall layout and design are by Colonel Mustard Design and
Illustration, Quay West Studios, Breakwater Road, Plymouth

British Library Cataloguing-in-Publication Data.
A catalogue record of this book is available from the British Library.

ISBN
0-9519778-0-6
Printed and bound by
BPCC Wheatons Ltd, Exeter.

CONTENTS

Page

Illustrations   7
Introduction   9
Acknowledgements   13

Chapter

One   The Lighthouse Men   18
Two   A Tough Life   28
Three   Collision   44
Four   Rescue at Sea   58
Five   Landfall   70
Six   The Bristol Channel   80
Seven   The Fishing   89
Eight   Ships' Masters   106
Nine   A Killer Disease   134
Ten   Changing Times   142

ILLUSTRATIONS

1. Frontispiece. A small Western Ocean schooner *Little Secret* lies on the tideline in Fowey - a port familiar to many yachtsmen.
National Maritime Museum London.

2. On Christmas Eve they signalled for supplies but nothing could be got to them. Line drawing. Rosie Fierek.

3. Scilly pilot gigs were famous for their speed and superb seakeeping qualities. Gibson, Isles of Scilly.

4. Small ships in Plymouth Sound, waiting for a windshift. 1858.
National Maritime Museum London.

5. The steamer held her course leaving them struggling in the water.
Line drawing. Rosie Fierek.

6. Trim was all important. *The Dispatch,* lightly loaded, running with a squaresail made from an old tarpaulin.
National Maritime Museum London.

7. The Barque *River Lune* stuck on rocks south of Annet (Scillies).
Gibson, Isles of Scilly.

8. A famous picture of Cornish looters at work. The *Voorspeed* ran ashore in a northerly gale near Perranporth.
Gibson, Isles of Scilly.

9   The rope slipped out of the score, throwing the men into the water. Line drawing. Rosie Fierek.

10. The beach was crowded with people, such a spectacle being a novelty. Line drawing. Rosie Fierek.

11. The Penzance lifeboat rowing out to the *Jeune Hortense*. The lifeboat's carriage is in the foreground of the picture. Gibson, Isles of Scilly.

12. A result of 'missing stays'. The *Lizzie R. Wilce* (nearest the camera) stranded near St Ives. January 1908. Gibson, Isles of Scilly.

13. Her sails in tatters, the *Olympe* lies abandoned near Mullion.

14. The crew of the *Hansey* were all rescued by breeches buoy after she struck near the Lizard. Gibson, Isles of Scilly.

15. *Garlandstone* lies quietly in her last berth far up the River Tamar at the restored Victorian port of Morwelham.

INTRODUCTION

The 'Turks Head' is the only pub on the tiny island of St Agnes in the Scilly Isles, and it was crowded. There were crews of French yachts over from Brittany, and from diving boats working on two of the offshore wrecks. English yachtsmen, were there in force, and swarthy Cornish skippers from the launches which had brought holidaymakers over from the main island of St Mary's.

Outside the riding lights of yachts bobbed and curtsied to the swell, and the flashing beacon of Peninnis Head across St Mary's Sound kept up its steady rhythm.

One of the Frenchmen started singing Frère Jacques, and marshalled all the others into their places in the round.. The voices in the pub swelled and rose, and then the pianist swung into a Rod Stewart number, "I am sailing stormy waters, to be near you to be free.". The tune was taken up with even greater verve, until the walls almost bulged with the noise and the crush of people.

Somehow it was rather moving; for in spite of the schmaltz, I knew that I had only to squeeze out of the pub, and walk maybe twenty yards or so round the corner, to see the great Bishop Rock lighthouse pulsating away on the horizon. Even closer, outlined against the starry night sky would be the dark silhouette of the now defunct St Agnes lighthouse, its white painted bulk acting only as a daymark for shipping.

I have been in love with boats and the sea for all my life - and quite why would be hard to say. I used to see them often enough on my way to Primary School, but this was deep in the heart of the Midlands, and they were canal barges and so can scarcely count.

The port of Holyhead has something to do with it. I can remember our holidays with Irish relatives, for we always used to catch the night boat across to Dun Laoghaire.

We would get off the train, and straight into what was for me a magic environment - a smell of salt sea, bright arc lights, the noise of shunting waggons, and sometimes if I was lucky, a rising wind. Maybe I was the only little boy on the boat with my secret prayer. "Please God make it rough". Nowadays I have the sense to add the rider - "but not too rough!".

The first boat I ever owned was a twelve foot clinker built sailing dinghy. She had no foresail, and the mast was stepped well for'ard in the bows. I fell in love with her at first sight, and if the vendor did not actually say, "Makes just enough water to keep 'er sweet sir", it was something very close to it. She leaked around the centre board housing from the day I bought her, and my best efforts to stop this were in vain - she was still leaking when I sold her three years later.

I have owned a number of boats since then - most of them small sailing cruisers, and have been privileged to crew in many more

Well, here at Calstock it is a quiet day in early spring. There is little wind around the house, and from my study window the upper reaches of the River Tamar show up clearly through a screen of leafless branches.

Garlandstone, one of the last of the line of lovely ketches built by Goss in his Victorian shipyard is there, lying at her berth on the Devon bank, in the museum port of Morwellham.

During the thirty years that I have lived in Cornwall there has been an explosion of interest in sailing, and a massive increase in boat ownership, and this has lead me to attempt a journey of discovery into the recent past.

What was it like to work in small boats which would not point up to windward well, which lacked auxiliary power and had no radios? How did the fishermen and longshoremen around the granite coasts of the southwest peninsula really earn their living?

I have gone to newspaper reports of the 1870s to see if their pages hold the answer to some of these questions; for this was without doubt a decade of major change in the lives of everyday folk.

Some of these were social changes, and others were technical. State education became compulsory, and telegraph communication, steamships and steam engines all brought in new people and new ideas. A steady trickle of holidaymakers was the harbinger of the annual flood to come, but in all these things one of course has remained constant. The sea has not changed.

Space has meant the drawing of some bounds, and so any stories about the 'Grey Funnel Line' - the vessels of the Royal Navy, have been omitted.

I.G. Cornwall. 1992

ACKNOWLEDGMENTS

Text from the Western Morning News and the West Briton has been reproduced by kind permission of their editors, and I am greatful for their encouragment.

Cover photograph, and photographs on pages 26, 73, 84, 121, 124 and 145 are by courtesy of Frank Gibson of Scilly. Line drawings on pages 23, 63, 97, and 104 are by Rosie Fierek.

Many people have helped me in the research and preparation for this book. I would like to thank the staff of Devon County's Reference and Information Library in Plymouth, and of the Cornish Study's Library in Redruth for their courtesy and professionalism. Also last but not least, Harry Chambers of Peterloo Poets, Ruth Edmondson, Neil Gallacher, John Gross, Tony Harold, Andrew Monks of Colonel Mustard Design, Mike Tillson, Helen Williams, and my wife Betty for her encouragment in so many ways.

A minimal amount of editing, mainly in shortening very lengthy reports, has been done to these accounts. Irregularities of text and syntax have been retained, because they give the flavour of the period. A number of the headlines are not original.

Western Morning News accounts are indicated by the letters WMN, West Briton by WB, and Western Daily Mercury by WDM.

For my father.

ONE

THE LIGHTHOUSE MEN

The Eddystone rocks lie some twelve miles out in the English Channel off Plymouth, and have been a hazard to shipping from time immemorial.

The Victorians were fascinated by any stories of lightships or lighthouses. Indeed most sailors of today, although they may be accustomed to satellite navigation systems, will still reach for their binoculars when they raise a light. It can then seem an eternity on a cold and wet night, wedged into a boat's cockpit, before the flashes are satisfactorily identified, and the bearing pencilled in on the chart.

John Smeaton's tower was the third one built on the Eddystone reef. This was in 1759, and his construction pioneered a technique, for it was the first in which blocks of solid stone were dovetailed in order to fit snugly together. The method better withstood the wind and waves, and this was important because calculations showed that at times the wavepower battering on the tower amounted to two or three tons per square foot.

His lighthouse was a great success; by the late 1860s however engineers were expressing concern about the stability of its rock foundations, and the debate opened about replacing it.

This though was the heyday of Victorian power, and there were those who had a more drastic solution to this problem - why not simply remove the rocks?

TWO MILLION TONS OF ROCK TO GO?

Mr Waddy asked the President of the Board of Trade if the opinion of competent engineers had been taken as to the practicability of blowing up of the rock altogether instead of rebuilding the lighthouse, and whether he would lay upon the table any correspondence on the subject.

Sir C.Adderley replied "Trinity House reports that the cost of blowing up the Eddystone Rock together with the rest of the reef would be ten times as much as building a new lighthouse.

"The Eddystone lighthouse which is situated between the Lizard and the Start is of very considerable use in navigation of the Channel so much that if the reef were blown up it would be necessary to station a lightship there...to obtain the safe minimum depth of seven fathoms which would be expedient in the unmarked approaches to a naval station at Plymouth, it would be necessary to remove one hundred thousand yards of rock, or one million seven hundred and fifty thousand tons, to which would have to be added the blasting of an inner danger at Hand Deeps, at present sufficiently indicated by the lighthouse. This would compute at another two hundred and fifty thousand tons, bringing in all two million tons which would have to be removed"...WMN March 1878.

At this time the press was concerned about the stability of the rock. A year earlier however, severe autumnal gales had caused it to ponder on the mental stability of personnel posted to the deep sea lights. It alleged: "They cowered in terror in severe storms."

Events at the Longships, built on the Carn Brea rocks about a mile west of Lands End, had given rise to this concern. Usually, given good visibility a flag code allowed simple messages to be passed from the rock to the mainland.

The off duty 'keepers lived in the whitewashed coastguard cottages on the cliffs above Sennen Cove, and tradition has it that wives and husbands could semaphore to each other.

In bad weather, before the invention of helicopters, the Longships must have seemed so near, and yet so far away. The seas off Cornwall's north and south coast meet around the lighthouse, and in severe gales huge waves, with spray reaching up nearly 120 feet to the lantern's glass, could often be seen smashing against the rock.

On this occasion the signalling code had been changed and although the flag flown at half mast indicated distress, the watchers on the shore could not decipher the nature of the problem.

DEATH ON THE LONGSHIPS

It will be remembered that for some days since signals of distress, and the flag half-mast were flying from the lighthouse...

An accident occurred on Thursday October 25th, when soon after dinner the housekeepers, Steer, Cutting, and Boyle went on to the rock to stretch their legs. The weather had prevented them from leaving the tower for more than a week. It was low water and the weather was fine. Boyle was full of spirits and fun, and was cautioned by Steer the principal keeper to mind what he was about or he would get into mischief. No sooner had this been said than the other keeper Cutting called out "He's gone over." Both rushed to the other side of the rock to try and rescue him.

They had got a rope under his right arm and at the imminent risk of their own lives drew him up close to the rock, but he was stunned and powerless, and was carried away by the strong tide from under their very hands, and of course they saw him no more.

This is the fifth mishap which has occurred at the Longships, and it seems to point to want of caution on the part of the men themselves, or to some flaw in the regulations. The opinion prevails that on highly danger- ous lighthouses like the Bishop, Wolf, and Longships, none but staid and experienced men should be employed. Young keepers coming from mainland lights being altogether unfit. In fine weather they take liberties with the sea, in heavy gales they are terror stricken of the frightful waters which blow over the tower...WMN October 1877.

Anyone reading the West Briton newspaper in 1874 could be for- given for sympathising with these "terror stricken" keepers. It described the effects of a gale on the exposed Bishop Rock Lighthouse, many miles offshore from Lands End, and on the very rim of the Isles of Scilly.

SEVERE STORM ROCKS BISHOP

During the gale on Monday last the Bishop's Rock light- house, which stands on a rock on the furthest south-west point of the Scilly Isles, was struck by some fearfully heavy seas. Two panes of the lantern were started, and the lens were broken in thirty places. The light-keepers say that when the waves struck the lighthouse, the noise resembled the explosion of a cannon. The seas on strik- ing the lighthouse caused it to reel and stagger, and on regaining the perpendicular it vibrated so that articles in the house tumbled from their places, and the lens fittings fell about the mens' heads. At half-past two on Monday a tremendous wave struck the spare light. The cylinders were smashed, and only two left to keep the lights in. The sand from many fathoms deep was thrown into the gallery of the lighthouse...WB April 1874.

Later in that same year a large party of Trinity House workmen had found themselves marooned on the Longships, and although they signalled for supplies on Christmas Eve, it was no use. They had to subsist on iron rations over the holiday!

PERILS OF OFFSHORE LIGHTHOUSES

Fourteen or fifteen artisans in the employ of Trinity House have been shut up for weeks in the Longships lighthouse, two miles offshore from Lands End. It was known that their provisions must be short, and some days before Christmas vigorous efforts were made to get them off.

The sea has raged round Carn Bras, the rock on which the lighthouse stands with such continuous fierceness that two attempts were unsuccessful. Packages of provisions were hauled through the surf from a boat to the men. On Christmas Eve they signalled for supplies, but nothing could be got to them. On Monday last the weather had moderated a little, and the Trinity steamer went out from Penzance and got the men off.

The same lull in the succession of gales, had induced some of the crew of the Sevenstones lightship to get their boat out, and endeavour to reach the mainland with a sick companion. The voyage across the angry water which keeps the mouths of the English and Bristol channels in a constant boil, was more difficult and risky than these experienced boatmen had calculated on. Several times their eighteen or twenty foot craft was in danger of being swamped, and they were compelled to bear up for Sennen. The Sevenstones boat was seen from the cove and a fishing boat put out and piloted the stranger in...WMN March 1873.

On Christmas Eve they signalled for supplies but nothing could be got to them.
Rosie Fierek.

One of the earlier mishaps had taken place in the course of a routine domestic chore.

LONGSHIPS DISTRESS SIGNAL

On Saturday morning it was seen that a signal was hoisted at the Longships lighthouse, and immediately a boat was manned at Sennen Cove. It was impossible to land but it was ascertained that Mr Smith the senior lighthouse keeper had drowned on the previous day. It appeared that he went to throw away some ashes and was either swept away by a heavy sea or that he missed his footing and fell into the water. At the time a dense fog prevailed and it is said that the first intimation the two other keepers on the rock had was the disappearance of the ash bucket...WMN February 1875.

Many suggestions were made as to how this difficulty of communicating with offshore lights could be overcome. An obvious one was to investigate the possibility of equipping them with telegraphic apparatus.

Such apparatus had been in use on the railways for over thirty years. The first telegraphic cable had been laid across the English Channel in 1850, and across the Atlantic in 1857.

Impetus was given to this idea, when during the early hours of May 8th 1875 the s.s. *Schiller* carrying 372 passengers and crew struck on the Retarrier Ledges which fringe the Bishop Rock off the Scilly Isles. Sadly there were few survivors to bear witness to the tragedy.

The Western Morning News was opposed to the provision of such equipment, and in June 1875 cited four reasons why it considered this would be a retrograde step.

It was particularly doubtful about keepers' abilities to handle such apparatus, claiming that they would be bound to forget how it worked!

TELEGRAPHIC COMMUNICATION TO LIGHTHOUSES

Owing to the wreck of the *Schiller,* and the absence of any means of making it known to the shore by the men in charge of the Bishop Rock Lighthouse, many suggestions have been made, amongst others that a telegraphic wire be laid between the Bishop Rock Lighthouse and land, and that a similar arrangement should be made in the case of other detached lighthouses. It appears that there are four objections to this.

The first, is that vessels would more frequently be tempted to approach the lighthouses for the purpose of reporting themselves, and thus actually run into the proximity of danger. The second is that a telegraphic cable would, in such a position among the rocks and breakers be liable to damage, and even destruction, and would at the best be untrustworthy. The third is, that the occasions when such a wire might be useful would be extremely rare (for it certainly must not be used for any other purpose than a distress signal), that from disuse the keepers would have difficulty in remembering how to work it; and the apparatus would be liable to get out of order. And the fourth is that the Marine Department of the Board of Trade has a new sort of rocket manufactured for them by the War Department; which the Department has named a "call rocket". It is to be used only when a ship is seen to be in distress and wanting assistance from the shore...WMN June 1875.

Nevertheless within three years the telegraph on St Agnes, one of the most westerly of the Scilly Isles had proved its worth. The small two masted schooner *Integrity* of Aberystwyth, had encountered severe weather and had sustained damage. The skipper's nephew was aboard, and in his blind terror he abandoned ship in a doomed attempt to swim to the Bishop Rock Lighthouse. (Other accounts claim he was washed overboard.)

Help came from Scilly pilots who rowed out and boarded her. They would have been using their famous six oared gigs. These were very fast, and guided by their skilled coxswains had excellent sea-keeping qualities.

Scilly pilot gigs were famous for their speed and superb seakeeping qualities. Gig racing remains to this day a feature of the island's scene.
Gibson: Isles of Scilly

SCHOONER BEACHED ON ST AGNES

The schooner *Integrity* of Aberystwth, Evans master from Lisbon for Wicklow, laden with a cargo of phosphate of lime, lost her foremast last Monday, and mainmast today and became unmanageable drifting about with the wind; and coming round the Bishop Rock this afternoon the captain's nephew jumped overboard to try to swim to the Bishop Rock and was unfortunately drowned. Some of the Scilly pilots boarded her and ran her into the west side of St Agnes with the stern part lying on the sand and the bow against the rocks. The stern of the ship was knocked in last Monday and the vessel is nearly full of water. The mate has an arm and a rib broken, but the captain and two men are alright. News of the accident was telegraphed from St Agnes to St Marys when the lifeboat was immediately launched taking off Mr J.Moyle surgeon whose services were greatly needed by the mate...WMN September 1878.

TWO

A TOUGH LIFE

Fifty years ago Harry Kemp sent a poem to Cassell's Magazine. He was then over eighty, and in it he looked back with pride and affection to his time spent under sail. Harry had been a deep water sailor, and his romantic vision might well have been varnished by age - or did sailormen indeeed take so much pride in their job?

> I am eighty years old and somewhat
> But I give to God the praise
> That they made a sailor of me
> In the good old clipper days.
> Then men loved ships like women
> And going to sea was more
> Than signing on as a deckhand
> And scrubbing a cabin floor,
> Or chipping rust from iron
> And painting , and chipping again -
> In the days of the clipper sailing
> The sea was the place of men.
> You could spy our great ships running
> White-clouded, tier on tier,
> You could hear their tramping thunder
> As they leaned-to racing near;
> And it was 'Heigh-ho and ho, my lad',
> When we were outward bound,
> And we sang full many a chanty

As we walked the capstan round.
Aye, we sang full many a chanty
As we drove through wind and wet,
To the music of five oceans
That rings in memory yet.
Go, drive your dirty freighters
That fill the sky with reek -
But we - we took in skysails
High as a mountain peak...

The romance of his memories is not born out by contemporary press reports. What comes through is rather different. At the best it is sheer grinding discomfort; at the worst an unrelenting drudgery, both among the deep sea men, and those in the coastal trade. There were times indeed when the misery of mens' lives drove them to utter despair.

The Western Morning News in July 1875 reported on the rescue of a man driven to desperate measures by bullying, and who sought sanctuary on a lightship! He was equipped with a bible and few pence.

SAILOR JUMPS OVERBOARD

As the steamship *Lady Wodehouse*, Captain Watts, was proceeding down channel bound for Southampton and Dublin, the lookout man on the forecastle heard cries from the water as of a man overboard. It was dark and raining at the time, and the vessel was about two miles and a half south of the Royal Sovereign Shoal Lightship, nine miles below the Beachy Head. The captain immediately had the engines reversed at full speed, and a boat lowered, which succeeded after a time in picking up a black sailor, who was taken aboard the steamer. He said that he jumped overboard from a barque, also on the way down Channel, in consequence of his having been ill-used, and that he intended swimming to the lightship which was between two and half and three miles from the place where he was swimming. He had a handkerchief around his neck containing a Bible and a few coppers...WMN July 1875.

Reports from the hearings at magistrates' courts give an insight into the bullying, sometimes called "hazing", which took place. Much of that recorded was on foreign going ships, rather than in the inshore trade.

Nevertheless, two of the following cases happened in home waters. One was in Plymouth aboard a small French smack engaged in bringing potatoes over from Brittany. She was moored snugly alongside the quay wall, and the ship's boy was the victim. He was having a quiet doze when his drunken captain discovered him, and kicked him severely "about the bowels".

BRUTAL TREATMENT OF SHIP'S BOY

At Plymouth Police Court yesterday H.Berbet captain of the French smack *Union* lying at the quay at Sutton Wharf was charged with assaulting Jean Mayon aged 13 years. The complainant through Mr Bellamy who acted as interpreter stated that he was a boy on board the French smack *Union*. On the previous afternoon the prisoner came down into the cabin where he was, knocked him down, and kicked him several times in the side and bowels because he had neglected to chop up some wood.

Eliza McCauley said that on the previous afternoon she was weighing potatoes on board the Union and at about half-past three o'clock the owner of the ship called her down into the cabin, where she saw the complainant lying on his back stretched out. After the owner went ashore the prisoner and a seaman came into the cabin, and the prisoner handed a bottle containing spirit to the seaman who drank some. After they had drank a good deal of the spirit, the prisoner kicked the complainant several times in the back and abdomen.

PC Stansbury said he went on board, and on going into the cabin saw the complainant lying on the floor groaning. There was blood about the cabin, and blood rushing from the complainant's mouth. The boy was insensible and was taken to the South Devon and East Cornwall hospital. The bench remanded the prisoner in order that the surgeon might attend and give evidence. The boy was taken back to hospital... WMN March 1875.

Dennis Farland got more than he bargained for when he too found one of his crewmates asleep on the deck. He started to kick him, but the man awoke in temper, and grabbed the nearest thing to hand for a weapon. It was a spade!

EXTRAORDINARY AFFAIR AT GUERNSEY

On Friday last, Dennis Farland one of the crew of the brig *Lilly*, finding one of his shipmates a Frenchman drunk and asleep, commenced kicking him as he lay on the deck. On the Frenchman gaining his feet Farland proceeded to "fist" him, and knock him about. This so exasperated the Frenchman that he seized a shovel and struck Farland a heavy blow on the chest, inflicting a severe wound. The wounded man was certainly the aggressor and provoked his shipmate (who is a very quiet man) to a great extent before he resorted to violence. Farland on having his wound dressed was directed by the doctor to go home to bed, but instead of doing so he went about the town drinking and exhibiting his wounds. The result of this imprudence was that he died on Saturday night, and the Frenchman is now in custody... WMN July 1879.

Captain O'Neil was skipper of the *Glen Monarch*, and he lost his temper when the ship's carpenter refused his orders, and climbed back into his warm bunk.

They were in St Ives bay with two anchors down. Captain O'Neil had a lee shore under him, and the sea was getting up. One of the anchor chains had just snapped. In court he pleaded justification for his subsequent actions.

SHIP'S CARPENTER ALLEGES CRUELTY

At Cardiff Borough police court today, B.O'Neil, captain of the *Glen Monarch*, and John Mylcrane mate, were charged on remand with ill treating Andrew Tarrach, carpenter of the said vessel. The complainant is a Dutchman who alleged that because he objected to get out of his bunk he was taken on deck and beaten by the captain and mate. His hands were then lashed behind him, and he was strung up by the arms to the boat's davits, his toes just touching the deck. For the defence it was alleged that the vessel was on a lee shore, and had lost her starboard chain and one anchor. Complainant on being told to get a shackle got into his bunk and would do nothing. He was consequently brought on deck and his hands were tied behind him. The captain considering that as he had such a rascally set of men on board an example should be made. The crew had had a month's advance, and all fifteen deserted at Cardiff. The captain was fined the reduced penalty of twenty shillings and costs, and the mate ten shillings and costs...WMN December 1879.

Nova Scotian ships were famous for their fast passages, and hard driving; but carrying heavy canvas in bad weather meant that their crews had to put in exhausting and back breaking spells at one of the most hated jobs aboard - manning the pumps.

This was overseen by bullying mates adept at dishing up "belaying pin soup", and these men were not averse to reaching for their revolvers.

Falmouth was the busiest of England's south western ports, and Falmouth magistrates were accustomed to hearing sailors' complaints.

In 1878 they had to hear a number of complaints which stemmed from work at the pumps. In the following a seaman alleged that the angry mate had smashed him across the face with a large iron bolt.

CAPTAIN ATTACKS SEAMAN

Linton Evans a seaman aboard the barque *John Brede*, of Halifax Nova Scotia, summoned the master Captain Washington Barking, and the mate James L. Forrester.

The complainant stated that on 15th June he made an innocent remark to the carpenter about two of the crew leaving the pumps. The mate who was standing on the pump well hatch went over and asked him what was the matter and the complainant replied, "I said nothing to you". The mate turned round and struck him with his clenched fist, knocked him down and kicked him in the body.

Complainant caught hold of the mate's foot and fell backwards. The captain was standing on the poop at the time, and called out. He then came over and struck him with his fist, he put his arm up to defend himself and ran into the forecastle...

The mate followed carrying an iron bolt called a "norman", and ordered him on deck. The complainant replied that he would not come up while the mate had that club in his hand. The mate then endeavoured to strike him with this "norman".

The captain at this point came in with a belaying pin which he eventually threw at the complainant and struck him on the cheek. This stunned him and he bled freely, and the mate afterwards struck him across the jaw and the shoulder with the "norman". On the 20th his face became so swollen that the captain ordered him to go below, and for six days he had poultices applied. The hearing continues...WDM October 1878.

The final case involves the systematic brutilizing of a newly joined apprentice. A combination of a weak captain, a sadistic mate and a cruel bosun seems to have driven the youth to his death. His relatives however were not prepared to be fobbed off with a 'Man Overboard' explanation, and they pursued the affair through three court hearings.

TRIAL OF MASTER, MATE AND BOATSWAIN AT FALMOUTH.
EXTRAORDINARY CRUELTY

Richard Proudfoot the master, William Strickland the mate, and James Murray the boatswain, of the barque *Maggie Dixon*, now lying in Falmouth harbour from North Shields, were on Saturday brought before Falmouth Borough magistrates charged with causing the death of an apprentice called Charles Astley Cooper, belonging to the same vessel...

Faita Rofoke cook and steward on board the *Maggie Dixon* was the first witness examined. The deceased was an apprentice on board and was shipped at Sunderland. He was then fresh and healthy. Soon after coming out of dock the mate commenced to shove him about, and in less than a week began to "ropes end" him. The mate was the first he noticed doing it. The mate told deceased at the time he had no business to come to sea and "take the bread out of poor mens' mouths". This "ropes ending" lasted for about six or seven weeks...

Witness saw it so frequently that he felt obliged to speak to the master about it, and asked him to protect him (the deceased). Up till this time he had not seen anyone else ill using him. After witness complained to the captain, deceased was not treated better, but was shifted from the mate into the bosun's watch.

On the third day the mate told the bosun not to give him a minute's rest. About the fifth or sixth day the bosun came down into the cabin and said that he knew a cleverer way of doing business than the mate did. He should not leave a ropes end to leave marks...the bosun after this used to kick him in the face and thighs with his boots on, and he would also strike him often in the back of the neck until it commenced to bleed, and the blood would "drip" out of his ears.

He was constantly bleeding like that for four or five weeks. Whenever the bosun met him he used to strike him, and when the mate's watch was on deck he was accustomed to strike him in the same way as the bosun.

Witness reported this matter to the captain, and told him he ought to look after the deceased. Witness told that captain he might ruin himself for life, and lose the ship and all.

The captain then went on deck and gave the mate, and bosun orders not to strike his apprentice any more. The captain then examined the deceased and had him stripped. Witness saw that he was black and blue with bruises, his body was not like a human being's ought to be. He had sores all over his body.

Blood was oozing out of his sores. The captain asked deceased where he got the sores from. He would not tell the captain at first, but he took a ropes end and attempted to hit him, saying "if he did not tell he would hit him."

The deceased said he could not tell the captain for the mate had said if he did he would give him another three dozen that night. The captain went to the mate and told him if he touched the boy again he would knock him (the mate) off duty.

Deceased was then left quiet for two or three days. After that the thrashing and beating about re-commenced by the mate, bosun and captain. The examination of the deceased's body by the captain took place about four or five weeks before his death. Deceased then got sick (which was about four or five weeks previous to his death, and it turned to scurvy.) The captain gave him a rope's ending as he said, "To make him learn what scurvy was". Witness saw the beating himself. This took place on the half-poop on the starboard side. The wheelsman was present, but witness did not know who he was.

That night the captain ordered witness to give the deceased double amounts of limejuice, and told him to mix up vinegar and limejuice to rub into the lad's sores, and to give him rice and barley. Deceased did not care about the barley, and witness gave him rice until the day of his death. The captain told witness not to give him meat, nothing but rice. "He would teach him what scurvy was, he would hunger his old guts out of him".

Deceased had nothing but rice, and what witness stole for him - a little bread to keep his life up for him.

The captain went to the forecastle and told the crew if anyone gave the deceased anything but what he ordered, he (the captain) would starve them the same. There were nine days to go, on which pudding was served to the crew. Deceased had it only two days at that time, with the exception of those two days deceased had only biscuit, and no pudding.

The captain then put the deceased down in the fore-peak to shovel coal, and because he took too much time over it he beat him. This was about a fortnight before his death. Deceased was suffering at the time from scurvy, he was to take the coal from the hold and put some in the forepeak. The captain told deceased he was not to have food until the forepeak was full.

Deceased commenced work at six o'clock in the morning, he got no breakfast, he came on deck at twelve to get some dinner. Witness had his dinner of rice ready for him. The captain came to witness and told him not to let the lad have any dinner until the forepeak was full. At one o'clock deceased came to the galley door again, but witness saw the mate.

The mate asked Cooper what he was doing on deck, deceased replied that he wanted a drink of water, he was faint. The mate said he would "faint him". He gave him a blow on the back of the neck, and sent him below. But while the mate and the captain were having their dinner in the cabin about half eleven, witness took a small bottle of water and biscuits down to the deceased. He drank the water, captain came down from his cabin and went slowly in to the forepeak, the witness following. Witness saw the captain look down into the hold and asked the deceased what he had there. Deceased replied "a biscuit". The captain said "Who gave it to you?" The deceased would not tell who gave it to him.

At eight o'clock the same evening deceased came into the cabin and asked witness for a bite to eat. He took two biscuits and put a little butter on them, and placed them inside the lad's shirt, giving him a little water. The mate came along with a cane in his hand, told deceased to hold his hands out and then beat the both. Witness counted three dozen less one. Deceased was singing out for mercy, to be left alone. The mate replied, "You little b— I'll murder you".

The next morning at four o'clock he found deceased on deck. He saw the sleeves of his shirt were torn, and there were bruises on his arm, after about half an hour he took off the remainder of his shirt to wash himself, and witness saw he was black and blue all over.

One of the apprentices threw salt water over him, the mate came along and said to witness, "..if you ever interfere again I'll choke you". Witness after that was afraid to say anything more. It was some time before this that the mate ordered one of the men forward to cut off deceased's hair and put tar and grease on. Witness afterwards saw deceased with his hair gone, and his head tarred.

The second day before Cooper died the bosun came into the cabin, (the carpenter, captain and witness were present) and after he sat down for his breakfast he said he would throw the "lunatic b— overboard", and "another one along with him". The captain said, "You must not throw him overboard, I want to see him home again to his friends. If he is thrown overboard he will be more trouble to me than all this ship and cargo."

The bosun said he would not think more of throwing him overboard than eating his breakfast, if it was not the law.

It was six a.m. when the captain came on deck, the captain took a rope and gave the deceased a severe rope's ending and ordered him to go from the deck to the main royal masthead, "Fifty times, before he had anything to eat". As deceased came down he counted aloud, the captain and mate were present. He commenced to go up the rigging about seven o'clock, and finished about a quarter to twelve. The rigging was wire, the witness saw his feet were sore. The mate on one occasion sent deceased to the main royal yard, to "sew his shirt", this was about four o'clock in the morning. Witness saw him then up there mending his shirt. He had it off, the weather was cold.

On the day of Cooper's death the mate gave his order to reef topsails. Witness just after saw the bosun shoving deceased along before him, and striking him in the neck and on his ribs. The crew went aloft to reef sails and the deceased went with them. Before he went aloft he looked like a skeleton, soon after (about five minutes) witness heard Cooper calling out, "Oh Lord leave me alone, Oh Lord do!". Witness went out of the galley and heard the captain sing out "A man overboard". Witness asked the captain, "Who is he?". The captain replied "It was Cooper". He pointed with his hand where he was, witness could see his face was bleeding, that was the last he saw of him. He was at that time two or three ship's lengths off....when Cooper was in the water the captain told him to bend on the lifebuoy, and throw it overboard to save him, but his body was gone too far.

Twenty minutes had elapsed before the lifebuoy was thrown over. Witness threw it over, and the captain was standing alongside the main rigging on the port side. The lifebuoy was out about half an hour. No boat was launched...

Charles Smith an able seaman on board the *Maggie Dixon* said he shipped at Sunderland, and the deceased had joined before him. He had been a sailor for nearly forty years. At first Cooper was in the mate's watch. He was brutally treated during the voyage. Witness had seen the mate drag the deceased out of his bunk naked, which was just underneath his own, and put him on look out with only a coat on.

He had also seen the bosun take him by the throat with both hands and dash him over the spare spar. Deceased could not go on deck without being so treated. He had seen the deceased with head tarred with all the hair cut off. The boy was very badly fed during the voyage...the mate frequently struck him with his boots, fist, ropes-end and rattan which he kept on purpose to flog the deceased...

Nearly every time Cooper turned into his bunk the mate used to throw salt water over him. He remembered when the deceased was kept in the forepeak from eight o'clock one morning until eight o'clock the next morning without any food or drink other than was given him by the crew. The deceased used to be sent aloft by the mate and the bosun and made to crow like a cock.

The deceased was very poor and thin and a skeleton. When an order was given to reef topsails the bosun and some other men were on the weather side of the mast and Copper was in the lee side. A little while afterwards he heard the bosun sing out "Man overboard". Witness remarked to the captain that the water was bloody, the wind was abeam. In his opinion he would have fallen on the deck or in the top. With the cry "Man overboard", he put the helm down. After about five minutes of hearing this cry he saw deceased rise to the surface and heard him saying "My God! My God!", he saw his head and face which were black. Only the captain and the bosun were on deck at the time. The captain called the mate up from below, and told him that a man was overboard. He himself went into the mizzen rigging - instead of throwing a lifebuoy overboard they stayed to bend a rope on to the lifebuoy, and before it was ready the boy was gone.

Witness said when the lad was stripped and washed he was also scrubbed with a coir broom...

Andrew Petrie said he was carpenter aboard the *Maggie Dixon*, and joined at Sunderland...he said he had seen the mate put the deceased into the lee scuppers and scrub him. All those charged were committed to take their trial at the next assize at Bodmin. All three reserved their defence...WDM April 1878.

The court was crowded throughout this preliminary hearing, and it was feared that an attempt would be made to mob the accused. However although a crowd of 500 people followed the prisoners from the Town Hall to the Police Station, they contented themselves with hissing and spitting on them.

All three were committed for trial at Bodmin Assize charged with manslaughter, and bail was refused on the grounds that the Captain might flee the country.

A lengthy trial followed at the Assize courts, and finally on the Judge's directions the jury found there was no proof as to how the apprentice lost his footing, and therefore a charge of manslaughter could not be sustained.

In due course however a third trial at Exeter in October 1878 found all three guilty of cruelty. The jury, somewhat curiously, decided that Richard Proudfoot the captain was the least culpable. He was sentenced to twelve months. The mate and bosun were each awarded five years penal servitude.

In the same year quarrels between Cornish fishermen and men from the East Coast were so bad that four Eastcountrymen were driven to ask for a safe haven in the lockup on St Marys on the Isles of Scilly.

The Cornish were busy breaking down doors in order to get at their opponents, and had to be threatened with the Riot Act before they would disperse!

A RIOT ON SCILLY

A riot occurred at St Marys, Scilly on Thursday night last. Some Eastcountry and Westcountry fishermen left the Atlantic hotel when a quarrel arose resulting in a free fight, and the report of what was occurring drew some Westcountry fishermen who broke open the doors and got in through the windows. The police managed to separate the combatants but about two hundred Westcountry fishermen assembled vowing that they would pull the house down to get at those inside. The police applied to the coastguard for assistance, but the officers could not act unless a magistrate's orders for the riot act had been read.

On it becoming known that the riot act would be read the fishermen dispersed and went to their boats. The Eastcountrymen then claimed magisterial protection, and four of the principal men consented to be lodged in the lockup until next day, when all being quiet they went to their own boat.

During the riot the hooting and yelling by the excited crowd was fearful. One Eastcountryman who tried to make his escape was seen and chased by at least one hundred men. He reached the pier first and jumped into the water and swam out of reach pursued by frightful yells from his disappointed and furious followers, another was caught on the sand and kicked and beaten very badly, and a third was knocked down and kicked in the street. One Westcountryman was sent home by the steam tug *Queen of the Bay* with broken ribs, and an Eastcountryman has it is feared a broken nose...WMN May 1877.

A different argument in the Western Daily Mercury ends this rather melancholy chapter, but on a lighter note. Watchmen equipped with powerful telescopes were stationed near the Citadel on Plymouth Hoe. Their job was identify and report on incoming vessels - however not everyone was convinced that they applied themselves to this task.

MISUSE OF TELESCOPES - PLYMOUTH

My attention has been called to a letter which has appeared in a contemporary, respecting the practice of certain men early in the morning, congregating near the Roundhouse on the Citadel, and watching through telescopes the ladies bathing - their excuse when spoken to being that they are looking for ships in the offing. This letter would leave persons to believe that this practice was carried out by the lookout men. I am informed on the best authority that this is not the case, and indeed that it is not civilians at all who do this, and that the men on the lookout have frequently had occasion to request soldiers and officers' servants to desist. It is only fair that the right parties should bear the blame, and a hard working and deserving class such as the watchmen for vessels, ought to be freed from the imputation of doing what all right minded persons would consider unmanly and contemptible... WDM July 1877.

THREE

COLLISION

One of the commonest forms of injury to both men and ships was caused by collision, and there are innumerable reports of these in the press.

It seems that poor watchkeeping, inadequate lighting with oil lamps - or no lights at all, very heavy traffic in the English Channel, and failure to obey the rules of the road, were four of the major factors contributing to collisions.

Basically seven rules governed the movement of sailing boats, and in the main they still apply today.

1. Close hauled boats have right of way over boats which have the wind free.
2. When two boats are close hauled the boat on the starboard tack has right of way over the other boat.
3. When two boats have the wind free, the boat which is on the starboard tack has right of way.
4. The boat with the wind aft keeps clear.
5. It is usual for the boat which is up to windward to keep clear of the boat to her leeward.
6. Whatever be the point of sailing, the overtaking boat is the boat which keeps clear.
7. Powered boats give way to sail.

Fortunately wooden boats tended to stay afloat, at least for a while, and crews from the vessels which came off worst in these collisions often managed to abandon their own ship and scramble safely aboard the other craft.

However abandoned vessels did not always sink, and their recovery, often by pilot boats which were cruising in the offing looking for trade, offered good opportunity for salvage money. At times this ended in litigation and acrimony.

The captain in the following report rushed up on deck half dressed, and then was so eager to evade responsibility that he attempted to pass all the blame on to the mate who had the watch!

To add insult to injury these unfortunate fishermen not only lost their boat, they also lost the money which was raised by sale of their catch. The "Falmouth outfitters boat" which eventually brought them to land, was one of the number of small craft which cruised off the approaches to Falmouth, and sold provisions, tackle, clothing and marine stores to vessels passing up and down Channel.

BRIGANTINE COLLIDES WITH TRAWL SLOOP

The trawl sloop *Esmeralda* 50 tons belonging to Mr Banks of Queen Anns Battery Plymouth, was brought into Sutton Harbour on Saturday afternoon, a derelict, in tow of the Falmouth pilot cutter *Antelope*. *Esmeralda* had a crew of three men and a boy, of whom two of the men and the boy were brothers named Hingston.

The sloop had been abandoned having been run into shortly after ten p.m. on Friday by the *Julia Daniel*, a three masted brigantine, Captain Owen Davey of Swansea, about midway between Wolf Rock and the Lizard. The *Esmeralda* had her trawl down and was standing under sail towards the Lizard, a fine breeze was blowing from the nor' nor' west, but the sloop was making comparatively slow headway through the drag of her trawl, and she had little command over her movements.

The brigantine had left Falmouth that evening and was standing toward the Wolf Rock, carrying foresail, mainsail, mizzen, two topsails, and two jibs, and was running at a high rate of speed.

The *Esmeralda* had her light at her masthead, and as the brigantine approached a 'flare up' light was used, but the brigantine's course was not altered and she ran into the sloop on her starboard bow, partially running over her, and pressing her down into the water. The trawler's crew took shelter aboard the brigantine, and on climbing aboard over the bows they did not they assert discover any person looking out, but shortly afterwards the captain rushed forward partly dressed, and the crew made their appearance.

Captain Davey in reply to reproaches from the trawler's crew said he had nothing to do with the affair as it was the mate's watch on deck. The fishermen assisted the crew in reducing the sail of the brigantine and then endeavours were made to clear the vessels. The anchor of the brigantine had caught in the sloop and two hours passed before it could be cleared and recovered.

When the vessels were cleared, Captain Davey at the request of the master of the sloop stood in towards the Lizard with a view to speaking to a pilot's boat because the sloop's crew thought that with such aid they might save their vessel. In the morning the *Norman* a Falmouth outfitter's boat was spoken to and the *Esmeralda's* crew left the brigantine in their endeavour to pick up the sloop, on falling in with the *Esmeralda* they found her in tow of *Antelope*, by whose crew they were warned off, as they declined any assistance.

The *Esmeralda's* crew were landed at Falmouth by the *Norman*, and returned yesterday by rail to Plymouth.

The Falmouth pilots found the sloop lying broadside with a large quantity of water in her, they cut away the road of the trawl and thus lost the whole of her nets, then they commenced getting the water out of her, took her in tow and brought her into Plymouth. On her arrival she was handed over to the customs authorities, and by their direction the fish found in the sloop, were as a perishable commodity, sold by auction on Saturday evening and made £13...WMN March 1876.

In a similar incident the unfortunate crew had been required to beg a small boat from their rescuer. The skipper agreed to let them have one, providing they signed a paper admittimg that they were totally at fault. They signed the paper!

They then discovered that a salvage crew from a Norwegian vessel was aboard their brig. This created difficulties, because they were afloat in a very small boat some miles offshore in the English Channel!

BRIG SINKS AFTER COLLISION

Before Mr Rothery, sitting at Poplar as wreck commissioner, with Captain Knox RN, and Captain Ronaldson as assessors, the case of the *Ethel* was brought forward.

This vessel was a London brig with seven hands, in ballast, and was on her way from Cowes to Casablanca on Monday 18th December; when soon after four on a dark morning she came into collision with a German barque the *Goethe*.

The crew of the *Ethel* took refuge on the *Goethe*, but at daybreak it appeared that the Ethel was still afloat. The crew therefore put off in a boat to take charge of her again, but before they could reach her, a salvage crew from a Norwegian vessel took possession of the abandoned brig and got her into Brixham.

The crew of the *Ethel* were then in some difficulty, the *Goethe* having proceeded on her voyage, and their own brig being on the way to Brixham. They were however picked up by a steamer and taken into Falmouth.

The master of the *Goethe* had refused to give the master of the *Ethel* a boat until he had signed a paper admitting that he was at default in the collision. Mr Noel Patterson appeared for the Board of Trade, and charged the captain with improperly abandoning the vessel. The court after a brief adjournment decided that in view of the darkness, and the apparent violence of repeated collisions with a much greater vessel than their own, the captain and crew were not to blame for abandoning the *Ethel*... WMN January 1877.

It is perhaps not surprising therefore, that when a collision did occur, the crew would prefer wherever possible to obtain assistance from known and trusted friends from their own village, or parish.

RUNNING DOWN OF FISHING BOAT

While the fishing boat *Aretura* of St Ives, but manned by a Newlyn crew, was fishing 15 miles SW of Bishop on Wednesday night she was run down by a barque, name unknown. The majority of the boat crew considered themselves in such danger that they climbed aboard the barque.

The captain of the *Aretura* however, 'Uncle Billy Mitchell', stuck to his craft and was hailed mastless but riding to his nets by a Porthleven boat. He declined her assistance preferring to wait until a Newlyn or

Mousehole boat came along. As this news was hastily given to the passing Porthleven boat there was some anxiety in Newlyn about the crew, but the general opinion is that they are saved, and that the plucky skipper who is over 70 will reach these Islands with his boat in safety... WMN June 1876

There were many occasions of course when survival after a collision called for seamanship of the highest order. According to the rule of the road at sea, Captain Dodd's ship seems to have had right of way, and he did not hesitate to risk his own life in an attempt to save his ship from sinking, after it sustained severe damage following collision with an unknown vessel. In so doing he broke his collar bone, and both thighs.

CAPTAIN BREAKS THIGHS

On Saturday morning the barque *Jane Avery*, 425 tons Captain Dodd, belonging to Messrs Avery and Company of North Shields, arrived at Plymouth with damage received in collision with an unknown vessel in the English Channel. The *Jane Avery* was on a voyage from Bombay via Mauritius with a cargo of cotton for Bremerhaven.

At 3 p.m on Thursday last when being about 40 miles to the southward of Plymouth she was run into by a vessel outward bound down Channel.

The *Jane Avery* was on starboard tack, heading east south east with a smart southerly breeze proceeding at about four knots per hour, and the strange vessel must have had the wind on port side and was going through the water very fast. There was a man on look out forward, the bosun was on deck, a man at the wheel, the captain was also on deck, and the lights were burning brightly, nothing was seen of the unknown vessel until she struck the *Jane Avery* a sliding glance down the starboard side, and within a few minutes was past her.

The hull of the *Jane Avery* was not damaged, but the following gear was carried away - lower fore topsail yard, fore topsail brace, fore brace, the upper main staysail yard, all the main rigging and backstays on the starboard side, the mainsail and all attached, the mizzen rigging, the rails broken and the dead eyes torn out. It is thought the anchor of the stranger must have caused the greater portion of the damage.

All hands were turned up and the main rigging was secured with tackles, but the wind increased to a gale and the hooks not being sufficiently strong were carried away. It became dangerous to go near the masts, at one p.m on Friday the mainmast and mizzen mast went over the side, literally rolling out of her, leaving only the foretopmast standing. At about five p.m Captain Dodd thought it would be prudent if possible to make fast the foretopgallant sail, but the crew considered it too dangerous to go aloft fearing the mast would fall.

The captain went himself into the topmast rigging, and tried to make the sail fast. In consequence of the heavy surging of the rigging he found it impossible to retain his hold and fell onto the sheer pole of the forward rigging on the port side, and then on to the deck, breaking both his thighs and also his collar bone.

The steamship *Arab*, Captain Brown, which had left Plymouth on Friday morning bound for Genoa, fell in with the *Jane Avery* in her disabled condition and took her in tow. She succeeded in towing her between the Eddystone and the Breakwater when the hawsers parted and broke the leg of one of the crew of the *Arab*, and tore off the tips of the fingers of another.

The *Arab* could not again take her in tow, but burned blue lights from ten p.m until midnight and continuously sounded her whistle for the purpose of obtaining the assistance of a pilot, but none came to her aid. The mate of the *Jane Avery* when the hawsers parted hoisted the foretopmast staysail and took the bearings of the Eddystone which bore southwest, and steered about northeast for the breakwater and fortunately succeeded in rounding the western end, and coming to anchor at about three a.m on Saturday without a pilot. The *Arab* was also anchored and afterwards landed her two injured men, they were taken to the South Devon Hospital.

Mr Fox, surgeon went off to the *Jane Avery* and attended to Captain Dodd who was in great suffering, and yesterday succeeded in setting the whole of the broken bones. The poor fellow was brought ashore in a cot, and taken to lodgings in Albert Street where he is progressing as favourably as can be expected considering the aggravated nature of the injuries... WMN January 1879.

In comparison the following court case seems to display an astonishing ineptitude by one of the parties involved.

Nowadays many yachtsmen are familiar with the problems of crowded anchorages, and will perhaps feel a twinge of sympathy for the skipper whose anchor dragged.

This led to a minor collision, but one which had serious consequences. *Acorn's* grounding on the point of the *Physician's* main anchor, pushed the fluke clean through her bottom. Attempts to winch free nearly ripped out a plank.

The Victorian press report makes the angry crews seem remarkably restrained, indeed almost polite, in the comments they passed to each other. The 'kedge' was a small iron anchor.

ACORN CASE HEARD IN PLYMOUTH COURT

The sloop *Acorn* having on board a cargo of limestone and sugar anchored in the Cattewater a short distance from Cattedown shore, on the afternoon of the 21st January. She was ready to sail the following day, and was anchored by an anchor and a kedge, and had her light burning all night. At about 6.30 a.m. on the 22nd January the schooner *Physician* hauled out of dock and anchored on the port quarter of *Acorn*.

The master of the latter immediately called to the master of the *Physician* saying she was too close, at the same time asking whether he had a buoy to his anchor. The other replied that he had no buoy, and that the *Physician* was sailing that morning. Almost before this conversation finished the jib-boom of the schooner fouled the boom of the sloop. The crew of the *Acorn* pushed her off as well as they could and the *Physician* veered out more cable, her helm was ported and that of the *Acorn* starboarded, and the vessels parted.

The tide was going out when the schooner came out, and between 11 and 12 o'clock it was so low that the *Acorn* grounded on the anchor of the *Physician* which ran into her bottom, and the sloop began to fill. Pumping could not get rid of the water and the crew having called for assistance from the shore did all they could to remove the sugar, but not before it was too wet.

The *Physician* being about to sail drew her anchor taut. She came close to the sloop, and the mate called out, "You are making a bad job worse, your anchor is through our bottom, and if you haul it out you will break the plank out and make matters worse than they are now." She desisted in this attempt, and the *Acorn* being lightened by taking out the heavy cargo and putting it into a barge alongside afterwards rose and the anchor was set free.

The court held the schooner was entirely at fault. She had plenty of room and should have given the Acorn a free berth. Owners of the *Acorn* were awarded £40-14-4d for damage done to the sloop. Owners of the cargo were awarded £120-17-4d...WMN February 1875.

Three months later Captain Dufruit a French skipper was not too far away from this spot. The sea was calm, his boat was lying quietly at anchor, and he was turned into his bunk no doubt hoping for a good night's sleep. A collision occurred.

The report gives an interesting glimpse into the problems of attempting to stem the inrush of water by passing a sail around the hole, (known as "fothering"). This was never an easy task, and it must have been even more difficult in pitch darkness, before the invention of electric torches.

His vessel was a sloop, a boat with one mast, and a fore and aft rig. This type of small craft became increasingly popular towards the end of the 19th century. It was easy to handle, and required few crew.

Fortunately his ship's boat had not been hoisted aboard, but had been left moored on his starboard side for the night.

COLLISON IN PLYMOUTH SOUND

The iron screw steamer *Tiara*, 1,190 tons Captain Bethel, belonging to Messrs Horne Brothers of Newcastle put into Plymouth Sound shortly before one a.m. yesterday...in the middle of Plymouth Sound she ran into and sunk the French ship *Jaques Marie*, a sloop which was lying at anchor with a masthead light hoisted.

The *Tiara's* engines were reversed with a view to taking way off her while anchoring, and the glimmer of the sloop's light was discovered right ahead. Orders were immediately given to go full speed astern, but it was too late to prevent colliding.

The steamer struck the sloop about amidships on the port side, but managed to clear her almost immediately. The shock was so light to the large heavy steamer that it was scarcely felt, and it was believed on board the steamer that little damage had been done.

It was then noticed that a boat had put off from the sloop, and shortly afterwards she sank. The *Jaques Marie*, was about 60 tons register from Granville, with 100 tons of wheat for Exeter.

Captain Dufruit stated that he himself and crew were suddenly roused by the shock of the collision and rushed on deck to find that a large gap had been cut into the side of the sloop and the water was gushing in fast. He had bare time to have his masthead light lowered and with it to examine the damage with a view to seeing if he could stop it with a sail, when he became convinced that no hope could be entertained of saving the sloop, and that immediate desertion was imperative.

Fortunately the boat was on the starboard side and was therefore uninjured. It was hauled up, and he himself and crew, five all told, got into it and pulled to another French vessel which was lying near, and on board her were hospitably entertained for the night...the loss made by the sinking of the sloop and her cargo is estimated at little short of 2,000, the sloop is insured for 20,000 francs... WMN May 1875.

In November 1879 over 200 sailing craft were sheltering in Penzance Bay from strong easterly gales. The wind moderated, and two of the skippers reckoned that it had gone down enough to allow them to weather the Lizard. They weighed anchor, and soon were both close hauled on the port tack. The schooner which was up to windward seems to have failed to give sufficient clearance to the brigantine.

Small ships in Plymouth Sound, waiting for a windshift. 1858. National Maritime Museum London

SEVERE DAMAGE TO BRIGANTINE

At about 5 o'clock on Saturday morning a collision occurred near the Lizard between the brigantine the *Gem of the Sea*, of Llanelly, Edgers master, and the ketch schooner *Star of the West* of Bridgwater, Davis master, bound from Cardiff to Charlestown, Cornwall with coals.

The brigantine had her bulwarks and main rail smashed, and carried away and her anchor. The schooner received serious damage losing bulwarks, stanchions, mainrail, topgallant rail, main rigging, fore-yard, mainsail, foresail, fore staysail, boom-jib, and springing her mainmast, and leaking badly.

During the collision the crew of the schooner jumped aboard the brigantine fearing their vessel was in a sinking condition, and assisted to get the vessels clear. Afterwards the crew of the schooner finding their vessel still afloat, returned to her in a boat belonging to the brigantine, and with assistance of the latter's crew got the vessel under command and bore up for Penzance, both vessels arriving at 5 p.m.

At the time of collision there were nearly two hundred sail at anchor, the wind being fresh from the eastward and the weather having moderated the vessels had got under way hoping to weather the Lizard. It would appear that both vessels were on the port tack, close hauled, the schooner to windward when the latter was struck by the brigantine on the starboard quarter...WMN Nov 1979.

The final account of a collision deals with one which took place in the autumn of 1879. The water must still have been fairly warm for Richard Johns was struggling in it for over fifteen minutes. He was by way of being an excellent swimmer - rather rare among fishermen, but was encumbered by heavy clothing and seaboots. (A 'hobbler' was the term used for unlicensed pilots, or for men hired to tow boats by rope from the land.)

EXCITEMENT OFF PENZANCE

An exciting occurrence took place off Penzance yesterday. A sailing boat named the *Janet*, with three hobblers on board was returning to the harbour when she was run into by a Plymouth schooner going in the opposite direction. Two of the *Janet*'s crew clung to the schooner's anchor and chainplates and eventually got on board, the third named Richard Johns jumped overboard - at the time the strong wind from the east was blowing and Johns was soon left some distance behind.

He was encumbered with heavy clothes and big boots, but being a noted swimmer managed to get off his coat, but could not cast off his boots. The occurrence had been observed from the schooner *Penar* of Hayle which was at anchor in the roads, but it was fifteen minutes before a boat could be lowered to get to Johns, who when picked up was just sinking. The *Janet* did not go down and she was afterwards towed to Penzance, but her crew strongly complained that assistance was not forthcoming from the schooner. Johns was in a very exhausted state on being brought ashore and appears to have suffered severely from his desperate struggle for life...WDM October 1879.

FOUR

RESCUE AT SEA

Richard Johns was engaged in his life or death struggle for near on half an hour. Two survivors landed at Falmouth from the *Estelle*, an American schooner, had struggled for over two weeks to stay alive after their vessel had been dismasted and swamped. One of them, Coseman, was washed overboard and sank, but he surfaced and managed to scramble back aboard the *Estelle's* hulk.

The skipper had ordered his crew to stream the drogue. This was a hooped bag made of stout canvas which was towed astern of the boat. The idea was to create a braking effect, slow the boat down, and allow the big seas to pass under the vessel. The risk of accelerating to near-wave speed was reduced, and so hopefully was 'broaching', or meeting a big sea sideways on.

SEVERE SUFFERING AT SEA

The Spanish schooner *Dorotea*, Captain Gary, from Aquaeillia which arrived at Falmouth yesterday for orders, landed J.H.Flat mate, and Charles Coseman seaman, who had belonged to the American schooner *Estelle*, which was commanded by Captain Horsey.

The ill fated vessel left Yarmouth, Nova Scotia on December 28th, with a crew of five men - and was bound to Antigua to discharge a general cargo. Immediately after leaving port she encountered bad weather, terrific seas and strong gales from the west south west, and had to lie to for three days under storm-sail with a drogue out.

On January 5th at three a.m. a terrific sea struck her and turned her over. At this time only one man Coseman was on deck. The captain, mate and crew rushed up from below. The other man was not quick enough and he was drowned in the cabin. The survivors managed to scramble on to the bottom of the *Estelle*, but Coseman was washed off, he was in the water for twenty minutes. He asked the captain to throw him a rope, but the captain could not comply.

Coseman then sank, but on again reaching the surface he got hold of a piece of wood and was enabled to get on to the vessel. After hanging on for four hours the cook became exhausted fell overboard and was drowned. At four p.m. the captain suffered a similar fate. In the evening the vessel righted, and the two unfortunate men managed to regain the deck.

The vessel was dismasted and full of water, and the deck level with the seas. They got a couple of narrow boards which they rested on the windlass and the water barrel, and on these planks they sought refuge during the whole of the fifteen days they remained on board before being rescued. For the first four days they could not get anything to eat, but after this a cask of apples was washed up from below, and they lived on the water sodden fruit, and some saturated salt mackerel. When they were taken off they had only seven apples left, and that morning at breakfast they had had two apples each and some rotten codfish. Early on the morning of January 19th they observed the *Dorotea* making towards them... Captain Gary sent his boat to take them off, and the poor fellows were in such a weak state they had to be carried from their own boat to the Spaniard's deck... WMN February 1879.

It was under similar weather conditions, again in the Atlantic in winter, that the small schooner *Albatross* of Jersey was lying hove to under close reefed staysail. It was Christmas Eve, pitch dark and blowing a full gale. Her captain was shortly to be called upon to exhibit seamanship of the highest order, and it passes almost without comment in this report. He was sitting on the companion way steps braced against his boat's motion, when the drama began.

MEN RESCUED FROM SEA

The schooner *Albatross* of Jersey, from Ganper for Jersey has arrived last night with loss of rails, bulwarks and other damage, having experienced terrible weather during her passage across the Atlantic.

The *Albatross* is a small vessel being only 79 tons register. At 9 p.m on 24th December when in latitude 51N longitude 34W, the night being very dark and a tremendous sea on, Captain Davis of the *Albatross* was sitting on the companion and heard a loud cry forward, thinking it was in the forecastle he ran forward, when he saw a boat coming alongside, and three men jumped on to the chainplates as the boat passed, and they were immediately pulled on board.

The boat which was under sail then went astern her mast being carried away by contact with the boom of the *Albatross*. It was then a gale of wind and a heavy sea running, the schooner was lying to under close reefed staysail. There were eight other men in the boat and as she drifted astern a distressing cry was raised by their more fortunate comrades. They were Italians and could only speak a little English.

Captain Davis seeing the great peril of the poor fellows hauled in the fore staysail, hauled aft the foresheet and bought his vessel stern on to the boat handed them a rope which the men fortunately caught and the boat was then fastened alongside, and the men and their clothcs taken out of her.

The rope was then cut and the boat cast adrift, there were no oars in her and the mast having been carried away as before mentioned, the manoeuvre had it been less skilfully performed the men must have been lost. It was then explained that they were the crew of an Italian barque laden with wheat bound for the United Kingdom from Baltimore. She had encountered terrific weather and shipped heavy seas and broken her bowsprit, smashed stanchions etc. The men had been six days lashed to the pumps and had abandoned the ship when foundering lower that morning. On 28th December the English barquentine *Loretta* bound from Baltimore to Caen was spoken to and eight of the crew were placed aboard her, the *Albatross* being short of provisions...WDM January 1878.

The crew of the small brigantine *Brisk* were convinced that in flagrant breach of all conventions of the sea, they had been deliberately ignored by another ship when they were seen to be in imminent danger of sinking.

WATERLOGGED IN THE ATLANTIC

Yesterday the crew of the brigantine *Brisk*, 280 tons were paid off in Cardiff. It appeared that the vessel sailed from a North American port on the 6th of last month with a cargo of deals. About three hundred miles west of Cape Clear the little vessel became waterlogged.

The extreme violence of the weather caused the eight men on board to almost despair of escape. For three days they were buffeted about by wind and waves. The captain, second mate, and Edward Small seaman were washed overboard, and were only with great difficulty saved. The mate's arm was broken, one man's collar bone was broken, and George Ewen sustained a broken nose. The lower topsails, and their shrouds, and the main rigging were washed away. The furious storm threatened to split the vessel in pieces. Once a brig was sighted, and this vessel observed their signal of distress, and hove to at about four miles distance; but then made off without attempting a rescue. Last Wednesday the Italian barque *Ida* came up and delivered them and they were landed at Cardiff by that vessel...WDM December 1877.

It was calm weather when the six men aboard the brig *Anna* saw a steamer approaching on a collision course. There was insufficient wind to move out of her track, and the steamer ran down the small brig, and then proceeded on her way without stopping to render aid. Four of her crew were drowned.

The consul general for Sweden and Norway was so incensed by the failure of the steamer to offer succour to the survivors of the collision, that he authorized the posting of a fifty pound reward in an effort to gain information which would lead to the identification of the culprit.

ALLEGED HEARTLESS CONDUCT AT SEA

The brig *Anna*, J.Nudson master, with a crew of five hands sailed from Santander on 19th July last with a cargo of mineral oil for Newcastle, but on the 22nd of the same month at eleven o'clock in the evening , when about 7 miles off Brest she was run down and sunk by a

steamer coming from the direction of the English
Channel. The master, mate, and two men of the crew
were drowned. The surviving two men who were
picked up by the Norwegian brig *Sarpaborg*, O.B.Olsen
master, had been six hours in the water clinging to a
portion of the wreck.

They cried loudly for help, but the steamer proceeded on her way.
Rosie Fierek.

They have deposed that on seeing the steamer drawing near, the helm of the *Anna* was ported but owing to the calmness of the weather the vessel did not answer quickly, and the steamer approaching at full speed struck her amidships and sank her instantly. The men have further deposed that on finding themselves in the water under the stern of the steamer they cried loudly for help, but that the steamer proceeded on her way without taking any notice or endeavouring in any way to render assistance.

In consequence of the foregoing the consul general for Sweden and Norway has authorized the owners of the brig Anna to offer a reward of fifty pounds to anyone giving information which will lead to the identification of the owners of the said steamer, and the conviction of the person or persons responsible...WMN September 1878.

Not all steamboat captains were irresponsible or heartless. The *Gelart* put into Plymouth, and her skipper reported going as he thought, to the aid of a distressed mariner. He was pleasantly surprised by what he found!

SINGLE HANDED MARINER

The Hamburg/American Packet Company's steamship *Gelart* which arrived in Plymouth yesterday, brought tidings of a man crossing the Atlantic from Cape Cod to Liverpool in an open whaleboat. At 2p.m. on Saturday, a small sail was descried from the *Gelart* steering east. Captain Barens at once changed his course by four points and bore down to see if assistance was required. On nearing the tiny craft it was discovered to be a whaleboat under twenty-three feet in length, carrying a gaff mainsail, foresail and jib. Its apparent sole occupant the adventurous navigator, was stretched out at his ease in the stern sheets, with his hand on the tiller. He enquired the longitude and having received that information returned thanks and the two very dissimilar crossers of the Atlantic parted company. As the boat had a fine favourable wind and similar weather has continued it is expected that the *Gloucester*, for such is the whaleboat named, will reach its destination today, if she has not already done it...WMN August 1876.

Alas not all sightings had such happy endings. The Western Daily Mercury told of the efforts of one skipper to rescue a distressed crew - but to no avail. It was off the Lizard on the south coast of Cornwall. This headland is infamous for fierce overfalls and heavy seas, particularly when strong westerly winds are blowing against down-channel tides. The sea was too rough to launch a small boat, so he attempted to float lifebuoys down to the endangered men.

DROWNED IN HEAVY SEA

Captain Kite of the barque *Archibald Feller* of Liverpool, arrived in Cardiff yesterday and reported that when off the Lizard, he saw two men on board an Austrian brigantine waving signals of distress. The sea being rough he could not launch a boat, but tried to send lifebuoys which failed to reach the vessel, and she foundered with the two men on board, one of whom was seen to be a passenger...WDM April 1877.

Samuel Plimsoll MP campaigned long and hard against vessels being overloaded, and in the end his campaign was successful.

The Merchant Shipping act of 1876 required a series of lines to be painted on the hulls of all British Registered Craft. These indicated the levels to which the ships could be loaded for different types of conditions.

William Watts was the skipper and part owner of a small brigantine, and had she been loaded in accordance with these regulations, his life might have well been saved. In the event he allowed her to sail only 18 inches of freeboard.

The account makes a very difficult task - in this case securing a top'sail over the main cargo hatch in a near hurricane of wind, seem almost routine.

ILL LOADED BRIGANTINE

An inquiry by the Board of Trade at Plymouth into the circumstances of the loss of life of William Watts, the master of the brigantine *Topaz* owned by Messrs Proust and Company of Swansea, about 180 miles sou'west of Queenstown, was held at the Guildhall in Plymouth yesterday...

Mr Kelly opening the case said the brigantine was of Swansea, and was 96 tons. William Watts was master, and owned four sixths of the vessel which was loaded at Runcorne in January with a cargo of pitch. She dropped down to Liverpool when she sailed on the 4th January, and was in good condition generally.

However the seamen thought when she was laden, that she was too deep in the water. At that time the vessel was in fresh water, and would not have the buoyancy that she would in salt water...

John Honnyman the late mate of the *Topaz* said the crew consisted of seven all told, including the master. Witness held a certificate of competency as a master. He joined

the *Topas* on the 15th December at Runcorne docks...
When the vessel was laden she looked very deep, the
captain gave him directions to load the vessel thirteen
feet for'ard and thirteen feet six inches aft; when she was
finished loading witness put his leg over the rail amidships, took a piece of wood and measured the freeboard
which was eighteen inches. The captain said, "You have
made a mistake, it is 22 inches." His opinion was that
the vessel was not well steered aft, and she was well out
of the water forward.

*Trim was all important. The Dispatch, lightly loaded running with a
squaresail made from an old tarpaulin.
National Maritime Museum London.*

They left Liverpool for Sette on the 4th January. The next day there was a strong wind and a violent sea. Winds during the voyage were very fierce and the sea heavy. This continued to the 22nd of the month. The vessel was wet, laboursome, and rolled to windward. She would not lay to. On the 23rd a gale sprang up, and increased in violence. By Sunday morning the 24th there was fierce gale, the sea rising and breaking.

It was as severe a gale as he was ever in, and by 11 a.m their boats were smashed - so crushed as to be useless, and the water filled his cabin. They cleared the water in five minutes, but the vessel continued to leak. She was put before the wind and run for about two hours, and then she was brought on to the port tack because the seas were over running her. A hurricane was blowing.

The main hatch was secured by a top'sail being put over it, because when the boat was smashed the tarpaulin was torn and the witness was afraid that water would go down the main hatch.

At three in the afternoon the fore top'sail sheet was broken, and the captain said that he would like the sheet to be furled. Witness went aloft, and three of the crew followed him. The captain was standing by the weather side of the deck, close to the mainmast. While witness was aloft a heavy sea swept the ship fore and aft, it swamped the decks and carried away everything movable.

The captain was washed overboard, and the mainsail and the stanchions were crushed. The captain was seen about twenty yards ahead of the vessel, but there was no means of rescuing him. There was a lifebuoy on board, but it would have been no good to have thrown it overboard.

The vessel was well found. If the ship had had a storm trysail she might have kept up better to the wind. The weather about four o'clock began to improve, and at ten o'clock witness ran the vessel for the nearest port he could find which was Plymouth...WMN February 1875.

FIVE

LANDFALL

Reports of ships sunk at sea are rather less common than accounts of vessels lost when making landfall in bad weather and poor visibility.

The jagged granite, and high cliffs of the southwest peninsula, took a merciless toll of victims - indeed a bedtime prayer of Cornish families is reputed to have been, "Lord send a ship ashore afore morning."

The small schooners, ketches, and smacks which made up the bulk of the coastal trade, either towed their ship's boat, or stowed it inboard if on a longer passage. In the latter case it would usually be cradled in chocks amidships between the masts, often on the main hatch cover. The boats were clinker built, heavy and difficult to launch in an emergency.

Catherine Griffiths was a newly built brigantine on a longer voyage though. She was en route to South America, and her crew had the terrifying experience of finding themselves in thick fog among the Scilly Isles. It was night, but visibility was so poor that they could neither make out the powerful light of the Bishop, less than three miles away, or the even closer lighthouse on St Agnes. They were totally lost amid the jagged maze of the western rocks.

Their first sighting was a mass of white foam breaking on the grey rocks of Gorregan reef, but they took prompt avoiding action, and must have heaved sighs of relief thinking that all was well. In the event only one of them was to escape alive.

WRECK OF *CATHERINE GRIFFITHS*

Our correspondent on the Scilly Isles sends these details of the wreck of the *Catherine Griffiths*.

The *Catherine Griffiths* was 326 tons register, commanded by Captain Henry Jones... She left Sunderland on the 25th October for Rio de Janiero laden with a cargo of coals.

At about eleven o'clock on Monday night when the fog was very dense the crew saw breakers against rocks which were afterwards found to be the rocks of Gregan lying to the west south west of St Agnes lighthouse. The ship was then steered by the wind heading nor nor west and going along at a rate of about five knots.

The crew immediately put the helm up hard in an effort to clear the rocks, but she would not keep off in time, and struck them about the waterline. She did not stop, and on sounding the pumps the crew found that she did not leak, and did not do so for half an hour after she had got clear of the rocks and was out in the sea and began to pitch a good deal, and rapidly made water which the crew could not keep under with pumps.

She foundered about midnight, going down head first and then entirely disappearing. Shortly before she went down the crew put the small boat over the ship's side, but she at once capsized.

They then lowered the topsails to get the halyards to endeavour to lift out the longboat stowed between the foremast and mainmast, but there was no time to do this, and several of the crew jumped into her as she lay on the deck in the hope of her floating off as the ship went down. But these seven poor fellows were lost. The only survivor is Giovanni Carstulovich a native of Trieste. He finding the longboat was jammed as the ship was settling down jumped out of her and sprang into the water and swam towards the small boat which had already been put over the ship's side.

On getting to her he found her bottom up and two of the crew, the bosun and the boy on her. They turned her over and got into her and on looking about could see nothing of the ship's longboat or of the rest of the crew. They had no oars nor anything with which to bail out the water and the sea kept washing into the boat. They drifted about with the tide and wind, and the bosun and the boy died one after the other from exposure, their bodies rolled overboard into the sea.

The fog was too dense when the ship struck and for sometime previously the crew could not see the lights of St Agnes and of the Bishop Rock. At about half-past nine o'clock on Tuesday morning the rescued sailor drifted ashore on to Troytown, the southwest part of the island of St Agnes, about the same time the longboat came ashore bottom up on the southern part of St Marys...the survivor said he waited until the last minute when he jumped overboard and joined the bosun and the boy, almost immediately the ship sank the seven hands on board all disappeared at once, longboat and all and no sound was heard.

The boy soon began to get weak and moaned in his despair but he helped to get the boat righted and got into her, the boat was again capsized, it took half an hour to right her. All of them got very cold and cramped and despaired of escaping their fate, the boy and the bosun fell away and died; at last he found himself in breakers and saw land near. The sea swept over him in that direction and at last he landed on some rocks. He got out out of the boat, held on with an almost superhuman effort, and got ashore and was saved after being nine hours in the water. He came ashore and was seen by a girl who told her father William Hicks, and so the

poor fellow received prompt and kind attention...WMN
May 1875.

It was four years later, at ten o'clock at night, again in dense fog
but with little sea, that the barque *River Lune* struck in almost the
same spot. Her crew took to the boats and got off safely. They
returned after daybreak and managed to collect their belongings.

She was in ballast for Ardrossan in Scotland. Her last port had
been L'Orient where she had discharged a cargo of wheat from San
Francisco. Her master Captain West, blamed a faulty chronometer,
believing there to be fifteen miles of sea room between himself and
the reef.

A small smack from Jersey had better though luck in freeing her
boat when she hit poor weather. She was en route from Brittany to
Weymouth with potatoes - at this time there was a steady trade in
vegetables from Brittany to South Devon.

*The barque River Lune stuck on rocks south of Annet (Scillies). Her
crew escaped safely.*
National Maritime Museum London.

EXHIBITION SINKS

The smack *Exhibition* of Jersey, 25 tons register Captain Moor, left Tregier with a cargo of potatoes on the 31st ult bound to Weymouth. At 10.30 p.m on Saturday when she was 30 miles n'orwest of Hanois light Guernsey, and while hove to for the jib to be changed, she was struck by a gale and immediately went over and foundered. Fortunately the boat was not secured on the hatches and as it floated off her crew got into it and remained until the next morning, Sunday at 8.30 when they were picked up by the French brig *Jaques Cartier* of St Malo bound from the Baltic for Marseille, and the same day at 8 p.m they were transferred to the French pilot cutter *Jeanne of Havre* which landed them at Falmouth yesterday morning... WMN November 4 1879.

It was a year later when the crew of a Falmouth schooner found themselves engaged in a life or death struggle, initially to free their ship's boat, which had frozen to the deck, and then to avoid death from exposure.

MEN ESCAPE ICE ON DUTCH COAST

The shipwrecked crew of the fishing schooner *Stour* of Falmouth belonging to Messrs Grey and Sons of Penryn have reached home and relate a very painful series of hardships.

The *Stour* sailed from the Isle of Wight where she was windbound for Hartburg in Holland on the 1st of December. She was laden with china clay. The crew were Robert McColl, captain, and three men, Vincent Rundle, William Sparg, and Charles White.

From the time of sailing they experienced thick weather accompanied by heavy snow storms and sharp frost. On the 4th December at midnight they sighted the Amaland light, and in ten minutes the ship struck on the Bow Reef, and speedily sank in deep water.

The night was very dark and it was with very great difficulty that the crew got out the boat which was frozen in a bed of ice to the ship. After being tossed about for two hours the boat was thrown ashore by three successive seas, when two of the crew, half-frozen as they were, crawled out and contrived to pull off their helpless companions who were frozen to the place where they lay.

They were quite helpless, and by daybreak not only exhausted but well nigh dead with cold. Immediately it was light one of them espied a landmark and finding it directed to a refuge for shipwrecked mariners they went there. They were kindly received and warmed but could get no clothes, after an hours rest a cart drawn by two horses conveyed them a distance of seven miles to the village of Westirchilling, on the way their wet clothes again became frozen on them. They lay huddled together in the bottom of the cart. Great kindness was shown to them and the doctor attended to the hands and feet of the captain, mate and one of the men which were badly frostbitten. They remained in their quarters here for eight days, and in consequence of the island being frozen in, the steamer from Haarlem to London could not call at the usual port.

On Saturday last they were pulled eleven miles out through large packs of broken ice to meet the steamboat. The captain did all in his power to alleviate their sufferings. The crew who are all Penryn men speak very highly of the unvaried kindness they met with in their sufferings...WMN   December 1879.

The Manacles lie to the east of the Lizard and are one of the most notorious of the Cornish reefs. Although reputedly from the Cornish, "maeon eglos" - "rocks of the church", their English name suits them well. They have held in their iron grip innumerable ships - including the *s.s. Mohegan* outward bound for New York. She was a luxury liner on her second voyage from Tilbury to New York. She struck at about eight o'clock at night. There was a heavy sea running, and it was dark. None of her boats were safely lowered, one hundred and six people drowned, and the captain's headless body was washed up in Caernarvon Bay some three months later.

Two ships had a happier ending on them though, they managed to get their boats away, and no lives were lost.

MANACLES WRECK - TWENTY-THREE SAVED

At about eight o'clock on Thursday evening signals of distress were seen and immediately the lifeboat *Mary Ann Storey* was launched. On getting out a large vessel was seen to be on a most dangerous ledge on the rocks called the Dolly May on part of reef known as The Manacles. The sea was running fearfully with a heavy ground swell but the lifeboat succeeded in getting alongside the ship and safely rescued thirteen of the crew which were on board; ten including the captain's wife, nurse and two children had previously left in the pinnace of which the lifeboat went in search. They found her a mile distant helpless having broken two of her four oars. They were also taken aboard the lifeboat and safely landed at Porthoustock, twenty-three in all.

She proved to be the ship *Ceres* of Greenock, 861 tons register, Captain Cocheran from Moulmein laden with teak wood and bound for Falmouth for orders. The rocket apparatus had been quickly got out from the

Arweack Coastguard station, but the wreck was too distant for the apparatus to be of service...WMN November
1877.

The schooner *Naide* though was a local boat bound for Falmouth.
Her skipper knew they were near the Manacles and was anxious. He
took the precaution of doubling the lookouts, and offering a reward
to the first man to sight them, but to no avail. There was a bell buoy,
but the wind prevented it from being heard.

WRECK IN FOG

During Saturday night and throughout yesterday a violent south west gale prevailed at Falmouth, among the
casualties reported is the loss of the schooner *Naide*,
Captain Peters of Gerrens, which occurred at 2.30 a.m
yesterday morning on the Manacles.

At the time the vessel struck there was dense fog, and
while the crew were getting the boat out, the *Naide*
filled and eventually became a total wreck. The crew
however succeeded in getting ashore in their boat and
were all saved. The schooner was of 122 tons burden
and was bound from Port Talbot to Falmouth and Truro
with coals. It was owned by Captain Medlin of Falmouth
and was British built. She was insured in the Padstow
Shipping Club, her crew have lost all their clothing and
effects. The loss of the *Naide* again suggest the desir-
ability of having a light of some kind on the Manacles
although at the time of her striking two men were on the
lookout forward and two aft. Nothing could be seen of
the treacherous rocks because of the fog, and the gale
prevented the bell from being heard...WDM Jan 1878.

There were times of course, when the elemental fury of the sea was so severe that it left almost no clue as to its victims - in the following account even the ship's dog was drowned.

PENZANCE WRECK

On Monday night during the height of the gale a three masted vessel with no yards, probably a French lugger, was seen off Penbarth west of Penzance. She had no canvas set except a staysail, and was apparently drifting towards the land.

The coastguard and others ran to the rocks and the vessel struck at the west end of the cove. There were no lights, nor could any crew be seen on board. The vessel immediately went to pieces, her mast, bowsprit, rigging and spars washed ashore in the cove, together with a small quantity of patent fuel, a dead dog, and a bag of sailor's clothes. On the bag was an anchor with the name Julienne Auray, a coat was found with brass buttons and an anchor on it marked "equipage de la flotte".

Nothing more was to be seen nor any tidings of the crew could be ascertained. At daylight a ship's boat was found washed ashore at Perrin east of Penzance, and marked on the stern *Alexander d'Auray*. This no doubt belonged to the wrecked vessel, and it is supposed that the crew left in the boat, and drowned on attempting to land. It is thought from the size of the vessel that the crew would have numbered five or six hands...In the channel a fearful sea prevailed, and a person living near Penbarth accustomed to the seafaring life states that he never saw a worse sea, and when the French vessel struck at Penbarth three successive seas smashed her to pieces...

During the height of the gale at about eight o'clock

last evening a French lugger ran into Penzance harbour, bound from Roscoff to Swansea with a cargo of potatoes.

The master reports having experienced terrific weather at sea. He states he left Roscoff with two reefs in, on Tuesday morning when about mid-channel he was obliged to heave to and fore reef the sail, when she filled herself on deck and remained under water for about ten minutes, some of the bulwarks then gave way and the vessel freed herself, but not before a great quantity of water had found its way into the hold, and had she been heavily laden the vessel must have foundered... WMN October 1878.

SIX

THE BRISTOL CHANNEL

One of the United Kingdom's busiest maritime thoroughfares was the Bristol Channel. The advent of the internal combustion engine and the lorry took away much of its trade, but prior to their coming it was the regular highway for many hundreds of small smacks, schooners, and ketches engaged in the home trade.

In the last quarter of the nineteenth century for example, Bridgewater, on the unprepossessing and muddy river Parrett, handled an average of a hundred and twenty ships a month, and many of these were locally owned small craft.

The Bristol Channel could never be taken for granted however. The combination of a high tidal range, swift currents and difficult harbours made it an area which demanded the greatest respect from those who used it.

FIVE LIVES LOST IN BRISTOL CHANNEL

During the gale on Tuesday, the *Fanny*, a ketch rigged vessel with a cargo of coal for Bristol foundered in the Bristol Channel off Clevedon, and all hands were lost. The *Fanny* left Cardiff on Tuesday morning, and when a few miles above the lightship the sea was so heavy that she was compelled to hail the steamer *St David* for assistance.

The *Fanny* then rounded to, and in so doing shipped a heavy sea, which flooded the decks, and sent her down stern foremost carrying down the only boat and all hands with her.

Neither men nor wreck afterwards appeared... Captain Webber of the *Ely* paddle steamer which plies between Ilfracombe and Bristol saw her go. "I was a little to the west of the Westhook buoy, between half-past two and three o'clock, with a heavy sea and the wind blowing hard and I saw a ketch with several sails set. All at once the staysail halliards of the ketch went and the vessel broached to. A heavy sea is supposed to have rolled aboard, and with the press of canvas she hauled over and went down"... WMN June 1875

The schooner *Gallant* was rather luckier; though even the captain's wife had to don her husband's clothes and take her turn at the pumps in order to help keep their disabled vessel afloat.

CAPTAIN'S WIFE HELPS SAVE SHIP

Last night when a heavy sea was running the schooner *Gallant* of Fowey, Norris master, Cardiff to Palma with coal, was brought into the harbour in a disabled condition by the steam tug *Victoria*, assisted by the gig *Lion*.

The vessel left Cardiff with one hand short, and had on board the captain's wife and child who is a boy of some five years old. The vessel was running down channel against contrary winds for some four days.

She sprung a leak on Sunday night about eleven o'clock, and the pumps had to be kept going. The captain's wife, donning her husband's shirt and trousers and taking her turn along with the men. At about five on Monday morning, the fifth day of their voyage they were at the Longships when the wind got into a gale from the south by west, which drove the ship back before it up channel along that coast of rocks.

All that day and the following night the hurricane raged. One after another they lost jib, staysail, top'sail, foremainsail, and square top'sail, while the captain was at the helm, and his wife at the pumps a wave broke over the vessel. It stove in the bulwarks and swept the decks, and the despairing shrieks of the child in the cabin pierced through the din of the elements.

Then off Lundy Island the main boom went, and the man under it on the spot had his arm broken by the shattered spar which was dropped on to him by a receding sea. In this state they were taken in tow yesterday by the *Vic.._ria* off Lundy and were brought into harbour...WDM February 1877.

In January 1878 the schooner *New Parliament* of Newquay bound from Kinsale to Bristol with a cargo of oats, put into Padstow. It was blowing a gale, and the *New Parliament* had sustained damage to her boom and mainsail. Her captain reported seeing a steamer sinking, the crew had retreated to the bridge, although judging by the newspaper report they must have managed to get at least one boat away.

STEAMSHIP SINKS IN BRISTOL CHANNEL

At about eleven o'clock this morning when twelve miles off this port the *New Parliament* passed a large screw steamer, dismasted, in a sinking condition and flying signals of distress. Her crew were seen on the bridge but no assistance could be rendered. About five this afternoon a boat containing several persons being rowed by four oars was distinctly seen from this place, she was trying to reach the harbour but was unable to do so, and was seen to be engulfed in one of the mountainous waves which was prevailing, all those on board have perished...WMN January 1878.

Like its namesake on Bryher, Hell Bay near Padstow is well named, and in north westerly gales is a magnificent and frightening sight. The *New Parliament* was a local vessel, and her captain knew the waters.

Later on the same day another craft attempted to seek shelter, but with disastrous results. The report is quite frank about the amount of wreckage obtained.

BARQUE WRECKED IN HELL BAY

A strong nor'nor'west gale having been blowing all day, and has resulted in the wreck of a large vessel and the loss of several lives. At about three o'clock this after-noon a barque which has been seen off the port during the day entered the harbour from the westward, the boat had some hours previously been sighted off Port Isaac running down Channel apparently making for this place.

She was under lower topsails and unfortunately for want of a signal halyard no flags had been hoisted at Stepper Point to obtain her attention and direct her to a safe passage. In consequence she kept a doomed course for Hell Bay on the St Miniver side of the har-bour, and soon afterwards struck. Her masts went by the board and breaking in two her timbers converted into matchwood in the course of twenty minutes or so. Only two of those on board got ashore, the rest nine in number being drowned. One of the survivors was the captain of the ill fated craft, the other was a seaman.

From them it was established that the vessel was the Austrian barque *Marco Primogenito*, Captain Banclovich...

The Austrian barque *Marco Primogenito* which went ashore in Hell Bay on Friday afternoon was from Glasgow bound to Alexandria with coals. Her pilot left her on the 18th off the Tusker. About one hundred tons of coals and sails, rigging and spars and other wreckage was secured on Saturday.

A famous picture of Cornish looters at work. The Voorspeed ran ashore in a northerly gale near Perranporth. March 1901.
Gibson, Isles of Scilly.

Quantities of wreckage comprising portions of cabin work of a vessel or steamer, some of it grained work, with grained wood panelling, others with white panels and blue mouldings have been seen floating on this coast. A hair brush with long hair attached to it as if it had recently been used by a female has been picked up, and also a red leather pocket case containing sketches and drawings of marine engines together with letters belonging to someone on board the *Lord Bute*, steamer of Cardiff. Through ignorance on the part of the one who found the case on Saturday it has not yet been delivered up to the Receiver of Wreck.

It is feared that two steamers beside the Austrian barque in Hell Bay have gone down off the coast. The steamer seen sinking by the *New Parliament* had a yellow painted funnel, white quarter boards, and seven men were counted on the bridge. On Friday evening cries from persons in distress were heard by Trinity pilots at Harp Cove. They put off in their boats to ascertain the cause but returned without being able to solve the mystery...WMN January 1878.

Local knowledge although a help, could not be a guarantee of safety in an emergency.

HEAVY NORTHERLY GALE. WRECK AND LOSS OF LIFE

Early yesterday morning the wind freshened considerably and began to blow from the north accompanied by showers of rain and sleet. At about eight o'clock yesterday morning a small vessel was seen running for Bude harbour.

It was blowing a northerly gale with a heavy sea, and the vessel being partly disabled missed the entrance, and drove down to leeward on the rocks behind the breakwater, where she soon capsized and broke up. The ill fated craft proved to be the smack *Maria* of Bideford bound to Boscastle with coals, Guard master. With very commendable promptitude the coastguard brought the rocket apparatus to the spot, for in this instance the immediate use of lifelines was imperative if life was to be saved, for some little time her crew clung tenaciously to the rigging, heavy seas in the meanwhile sweeping over the vessel from one end to the other.

The position of the poor fellows was a very desperate one, from her crosstrees one man was saved by means of a rope cut from an adjoining wreck and thrown to him by those who arrived first on the outer edge of the reef where the vessel struck.

The captain was lower down in the rigging and he went over with the vessel as he capsized. Several lines were in use on the spot, and it is said that two lay across the captain's back as he was in the water still clinging to the rapidly diminishing wreck. The only thought is that Captain Guard must have been entangled amidst the rigging of the floating wreck, for he once had a line in his hand - his body has not been washed up ashore this evening as it is still blowing a hard northerly gale with blinding hail showers... WMN March 1877.

It was only a few months later that the tiny fishing village of Clovelly was mourning the loss in the Bristol Channel of four of its most experienced sailors.

The *Rose of Torridge* was one of many small westcountry schooners engaged in the Newfoundland trade. She had been built by George and John Cox in their yard at Cleave Houses near Bideford.

She sailed regularly to Newfoundland, from Bideford and from Portmadoc. Her cargoes were dried fish, usually salted cod, from Newfoundland to Europe, and she returned laden with cargoes of wine or salt.

This account gives an insight into the local knowledge of currents and tides off the north Devon coast, and highlights the slowness of communications prior to the introduction of wireless telephony.

It also illustrates once again how communities pulled together in times of trouble.

SCHOONER *ROSE OF TORRIDGE*

The schooner *Rose of Torridge* came into Clovelly Roads on Saturday evening May 5th, and remained until the following Monday. The captain and mate are brothers, inhabitants of Clovelly. On the Monday at about 2 p.m they were about to leave and get under way for Cadiz. Four men viz Captain James Bate, Captain William Burman, Mr William Pengelly, and Mr W.Jones-Pengelly, put off in a small punt called *Victory*, to assist in weighing anchor.

It is feared that having got the vessel underway they remained on board, and the time and the place of leaving the vessel can not be known until the *Rose of Torridge* reaches her port. During Monday night great anxiety prevailed at finding the boat had not returned, and at 3 a.m on Tuesday a boat was manned by a volunteer crew who rowed as far as Hartland Point, and the searching boat returned at about 8.30 a.m but without any tidings as to the missing men and boat.

It was thought by some of the sailors the punt after leaving the vessel might have become disabled and so drifted towards Lundy, and the skiff *Wave* of Clovelly was therefore started for that island, it returned about midnight the search having proved fruitless. During Tuesday, Wednesday and Thursday conjectures as to what had become of the ill fated men, and sad gloom could be seen on the brows of the inhabitants.

On Thursday evening at about 6 o'clock a telegram was received from Salcombe stating that the captain of the schooner *Idris* had picked up the missing boat off Hartland Point on Tuesday evening at about 10 o'clock, it was in the right position but was full of water. It became evident that by some means it had upset after leaving the vessel. The missing men are all greatly respected in Clovelly, and with the exception of Mr Jones-Pengelly, were married, but two leave no family...WMN May 1877.

SEVEN

THE FISHING

Gales, collisions and strandings provided dramatic headlines; but it was fishing which took a steady toll from those attempting to earn a precarious living around the coasts of the south-west peninsula. Many fishermen could not swim, and although cork life saving gear was available few fishermen could afford to buy it.

FATAL ACCIDENT BEFALLS PLYMOUTH FISHING BOAT

A fatal accident befell a Plymouth fishing boat between three and four o'clock on Saturday morning. The boat *Membry*, belonging to Mr Edward Fisher, was returning from fishing grounds off the port with a load of fish for the market when the boat was capsized in a squall and sunk between the Breakwater lighthouse and Picklecombe Point.

There were on board her owner and his three sons, aged nineteen, sixteen and fourteen. When the squall sprang up the eldest lad was at the halyards of the fore-sail which were let go, and the lug run down. The after part of the boat was very low in the water and as she heeled over by the sail filling, a heavy sea poured in abaft and she went down stern foremost.

The father secured two oars and passed them one each to his younger lads, the eldest lad caught hold of two small boards which floated out of the boat, the father and his sons were for several minutes floating near each other. They were much exhausted by the coldness of the water, and by their endeavours to keep afloat, encumbered by their heavy boots and oilskin clothes they wore.

They kept encouraging each other to struggle for life, but Fisher at length called out that he could not keep up much longer. The youngest lad who was very near his father called to him to hold on for two or three minutes as he saw a boat making towards them, but Fisher made no reply and a few minutes after he was missed, having sank.

The two fishing sloops of the port, the *Almera*, and the *John and Sarah* were also running in with their catches, heard the cries of the lads and bore down to their rescue. The *Almera* picked up one and the *John and Sarah* the other two.

All the lads had had a very narrow escape as they felt assured that they could not have kept themselves afloat only a few minutes longer. The eldest had at first his face to the sea and was being fast exhausted by the wash of the sea against him, but fortunately he had the presence of mind to shift his position so as to be drifting before the sea.

With the many appliances which can be obtained for the rescue of life under such circumstances life buoys, life collars, or a few pounds of cork would do much to preserve life. Fisher was forty-five years of age, and in addition to the three lads leaves a widow and daughter.

The family will depend on the earnings of this boat which was swept for on Saturday and some of the nets recovered, but as she had a quantity of ballast on board, the services of a diver will be necessary...WMN February 1877.

The Royal National Lifeboat Institution had mounted a campaign to persuade ship-owners to fit out their craft with lifesaving gear - and this met with some success as the West Briton reported in March 1873.

SEAMENS' LIFEBELTS

The owners of the following Penzance schooners have supplied their crews with life-belts, procured from the Royal National Lifeboat Institution:- *Prima Donna, Gazelle, Mary Jane, Lafrowda, and Tell-Tale.* We hope that the excellent example will be followed by other ship-owners. The expense is not serious, and the pre-caution is very likely to result in the saving of life, when no other means are available... WB March 1873.

Events threatening fishermens' lives were not always dramatic. John and William Sweet from Port Quin on the rugged north coast of Cornwall were picking mussels.

DANGER TO MUSSEL

A few days since John and William Sweet, of Port Quin went to pick mussels on the rocks just by, there being pretty much ground sea at the time. William Sweet per-ceived a large wave approaching, and at once grasped a rock for succour, calling on his brother to do the same. On the retreat of the wave, the basket of poor 'Joyce' was observed floating, but he himself was nowhere to be seen, and at this date, June 25, the body has not been found. This is the fifth calamity which has fallen on this family within the last few months...WB June 1872.

Mousehole is a tiny village near Newlyn. The harbour is constructed from two breakwaters, and these leave an entrance of only 11 metres wide. In strong onshore winds this can be closed with balks of timber. It was not quite rough enough for this in January 1875 - but the fishing community was not expecting the return of one of their boats, and so problems arose.

LOSS OF MOUNTS BAY FISHING BOAT

A fatal accident occurred at Mousehole, three miles west of Penzance on Friday night by which two lives were lost.

The fishing boat *Robert Young* was returning from Plymouth herring fishery, and at about 9 o'clock of the evening arrived off Mousehole harbour. At the time it was blowing strongly with a rather heavy surf, the tide being at half-ebb.

The *Robert Young* made the harbour all right, and the crew evidently expected some of the fishermen to be on the pier to whom they might throw a rope. It being a dark and a dismal night and no boats expected there were no men on the quay. Consequently the boat having got to the mouth of the small harbour was washed out again by the surf to the back of the pier, before aid could be given by the fishermen on the shore who were almost immediately on the spot.

Ropes were thrown to the boat and every attention given to saving her, the crew evidently thinking their own safety was all right. But in this they were mistaken for all efforts to get the boat into the pier were unavailing and she got into the surf broadside on.

Andrew Eddy of St Buryan aged 22 was not well, and being weak and feeble got washed overboard and perished; and Edgar Tonkins a lad of 15, apparently got entangled in the ropes and was pulled overboard and drowned.

The remaining four men with much difficulty were saved by means of ropes, and were drawn up over the back of the pier. Eddy was picked up soon after the incident, and the lad on Saturday morning. The nets and materials were got out of the boat, and she was dragged to the mouth of the harbour but went to pieces there. She was not insured...WMN January 1875.

Lacking engines, and with almost no means of communicating with the land, small fishing boats were always at the mercy of a sudden and unexpected change in the weather. The whole community would worry when one of its boats was caught out.

GALLANT ACT AT HALLSANDS

At about midday on Thursday three boats each containing two men put out from Hallsands for the purpose of getting bait. In a few hours afterwards a violent thunderstorm came on, darkness approached and no boats returned to the village.

The villagers became alarmed and sent messages to Torcross whence they telegraphed to Brixham asking whether the missing ones were there. The reply was to the effect that only one of the three boats had put in at Brixham, but at about eight o'clock another boat returned to Beesands, a mile and a half from Hallsands.

One boat was still missing...almost all the inhabitants of Hallsands were on the beach gazing seaward...the watchers were at length rewarded for at about ten o'clock a flash of lightning gave a momentary view of the boat.

It was evident that her two occupants could not land unassisted. Dogs are trained at Hallsands to swim out to returning boats and bring ashore ropes whereby the villagers male and female drag them high and dry on to the beach. Now however the dogs were frightened by the lightning and refused to go into the water.

Hope was fast giving way to despair when a young artist who had recently come to the village appeared on the scene, stripped off some of his clothing and plunged into the sea. He proved to be a magnificent swimmer, but the general opinion of the spectators was that he would never return alive. He did return however but with very great difficulty and brought with him a rope whereby the boat was drawn ashore and the men restored to their anxious friends...WDM August 1876.

The far south-west of Cornwall was noted for its mackerel and pilchard fisheries, but sometimes there would be a spell of poor catches, and then whole communities suffered. The natural reaction when the shoals came back again was to catch as many as possible - this often overloaded the small boats, with disastrous results.

FOUR FISHERMEN DROWN AT PORT ISAAC

A distressing boat accident happened here on Friday night. During the afternoon very large numbers of pilchards were observed travelling westwards, and not withstanding the heavy ground sea and coarse weather the boats hurried out and 'shot' during the afternoon. Every boat was stow laden, and in most cases the fishermen had to leave part of their nets behind.

The *Lochan* was observed bailing about a mile from here and it is supposed that she must have taken too many fish aboard as she has not arrived. She must have sunk with her crew which consisted of Robert Blake, Thomas Parson, William Sleep, and William Inch. Blake leaves a widow and four children unprovided for - the boat and nets were his own, Thomas and Sleep also leave widows. The lifeboat was out for some hours during the night, but no sign of the boat could be found. Many other boats had narrow escapes through being so heavily laden... WDM December 1877.

Six years earlier history had been made when the Union Company at St Ives had enclosed in one of its largest seine nets a truly massive haul of pilchards.

A seine net was rather like a gigantic curtain hanging down in the sea and when both ends were drawn together, the fish were trapped inside it.

The 1871 pilchard season was one of the best on record, and in contrast to the years of near poverty, some reports claim that earnings of fishermen the St Ives area totalled over £30,000. Women and children were employed at 3d an hour in packing the pilchards into layers of salt, and thousands of hogsheads of pilchards were exported to Spain and Italy.

It is doubtful whether the fishermens' profits actually reached the reported figures, because the glut of fish resulted in prices falling to an all time low, and unwanted cargoes were brought back from Italy and purchased for manure.

MASSIVE HAUL OF PILCHARDS

Today's news comprises an incident which we believe is without parallel in the history of our fishery. At St Ives the Union Company enclosed on Saturday one of the largest shoals, if not the very largest ever captured. It was at Carrick Gladden, and not a moment was lost in dipping the tuck-net into the seething mass of fish, variously estimated at from 5,000 to 10,000 hogsheads. By hard work, continuing into the Sunday morning 1,000 hogsheads were secured. This morning operations were to be resumed when it was found, that owing to the density of the shoal and the shallowness of the water, thousands of hogsheads were dead. They lay in masses four or five feet deep - enough to be placed in a line from St Ives to John O'Groats and back again, and now instead of being cured into wholesome food for the Italians, they are now only "mun", or manure, worth 7s. or 8s. a cartload...WB October 1871.

Many of the accidents which put fishermens' lives at risk were quite undramatic ones, both of the following reports are from Brixham.

BRIXHAM FISHERMEN ESCAPE

Seven Brixham fishermen had a narrow escape from drowning on Saturday evening when engaged in the outer harbour in recovering an anchor and chain which was left by the fishing ketch *Nebraska* in the gale on November 24th. The men had succeeded in getting hold of the chain with a grapnel and were bringing it over the stern of the boat when the rope on which they were pulling slipped out of the score and sliding to the side of the boat immediately turned her over throwing the occupants into the water. Fortunately there was another boat near and towards this those who could swim struck out and getting into her they picked up their comrades...WDM December 1877.

The rope slipped out of the score, throwing the men into the water.

NARROW ESCAPE AT BRIXHAM

A trawling lad named James Cane had a narrow escape from drowning at Brixham on Saturday morning. He was sculling a boat towards the fishmarket when his oar slipped and he fell overboard. He soon sank amidst the cries of spectators. A trawler named Samuel Tucker gallantly plunged in after him, and succeeding in sustaining him until picked up by the boat of the *Peto*. Whilst the excitement was at its height an elderly woman named Mary Leach being hurried along by the crowd fell and broke one of her arms...WMN October 1876.

Fish buyers played a crucial role in determining the earnings of the fishermen. The latter lacking proper refrigeration facilities were unable to hold out when cartels offered low prices. Billingsgate was London's major fish market. Its opinion of some catches was forthright and important.

MOUNTS BAY MACKEREL FISHERY

The *Guide* arrived from the islands of Scilly at nine o'clock with a hundred and forty seven pads and left again at eleven. Boats arrived at Newlyn throughout the evening and night, and again this morning with quantities varying from 5,000 to 2,000. An East country boat brought to Penzance 8,000 which sold at eight shillings per hundred. We are sorry to hear that the quality of these latest catches is not so good, and that fish have arrived at Billingsgate in poor condition, so as to be described as "dung", "muck" etc, with a request to send no more, unless the saleable condition can be improved. One Mounts Bay boat arrived this afternoon with 2,000, another with 4,000 fish which sold at a better price. Damaged mackerel were retailed at 24 for a shilling. The buyers speak of the last catches as being the wrong sort altogether. They are too young and small, and so tender that there is no getting them to market, even iced in good plight...WDM June 1873.

Cooperation and self help were not always the order of the day amongst the fishing communities though, and there were times when quarreling and ill feeling were so strong, that the Admiralty was reduced to sending a gun boat down from Plymouth in an attempt to see that order and regulations were kept.

The Western Daily Mercury of April 1877 commented on the problem of nets being damaged by selfish skippers of schooners.

NEWLYN WEST FISHERIES

A petition to John St Aubyn as the member for West Cornwall, numerously signed by Newlyn fishermen complaining of violations of the deep sea fisheries act and asking him to bring the matter before the authorities was forwarded on Wednesday last. It was seen that considerable injury has during the last few nights, been done to the nets of drift fishermen by trawlers illegally passing by night over the nets on the drift fishing grounds. It is hoped the Admiralty would send a gunboat to enforce the law in the Mounts Bay fisheries during this mackerel season. But the expectation proved fallacious, and considerable and serious injury has thereby ensued to many hard working and industrious men. It is hoped that this memorial may produce some effect...WDM April 1877.

Damage to fishing occurred in other ways though, and an investigation in the same year listened to an account which a witness claimed "frightened him to see the effects". Many tin miners eked out their living with casual fishing.

Sometimes though, as the report suggests there was friction between these two groups. It resulted in a public inquiry in May 1877.

CATCHING FISH WITHOUT BAIT

About eighteen months ago John Ellis who practices as a Sennen Cove fisherman was invited by his uncle a miner and a fisherman to "Come up and spend the day and see how to catch fish without baits". Ellis went, and saw a charge of dynamite thrown amongst shoals of bass, and to use his words at the public inquiry in the Penzance Town Hall on Friday, he was "frightened to see the effects, and he never wished to see similar fishing."

He spread the news among his neighbours in Sennen Cove, and they have since watched and tested dynamite fishing. Their opinion is so strongly and unanimously against it (aided as they were in bringing their views before the Secretary of State by gentlemen from the neighbourhood, and from Falmouth) that it has had considerable influence in securing this current inquiry. The investigation was attended by fifty or sixty fishermen and by several seine owners...WDM May 1877.

A fishing lugger *Band of Hope*, of Mevagissey, came into even closer contact with explosives, at least according to the accounts of those on board.

FISHING BOAT UNDER FIRE

The fishing lugger *Band of Hope*, owned by Mr M.Dunn, Mevagissey was on her way to Plymouth a few days since with a quantity of mackerel, and before entering the Sound passed the line of fire of one of her Majesty's ironclad ships, which was out for shot and shell practice. All proceeded well for a little, when suddenly a shot whisted over the lugger in such proximity as to frighten the unfortunate crew nearly out of their wits. Their mental condition was not all improved by a shell following the shot, and which bursting scattered its fragments in every direction; but on the contrary, every man instantly fell on his face, and according to their own story, expected the next minute to be ushered out of existence...WB May 1871.

Lack of insurance, and loss of earnings in the event of an accident to the wage earner were constant worries in the fishing industry. Charity in the form of assistance from Friendly Societies, or aid from public subscriptions were often the only methods open to communities when they were faced with this problem.

BOAT ACCIDENT AT TEIGNMOUTH

The cases of the widows and orphans of Charles Pitwood and James Scanell, the two fishermen recently drowned off Teignmouth were the subject of a public meeting in that town on Saturday. A committee was appointed for the purpose of obtaining subscriptions, and several amounts were promised in the room.

It was determined that five pounds each should be given to Soper and Paddon, the two men who were rescued, for the loss they had sustained, and because of their inability to again work as fishermen in consequence of the exposures to which they had been subjected...

A report reached Budleigh Salterton on Friday that herring fishermen had found the gear belonging to the Teignmouth fishermen who drowned some time since. It was believed that the bodies of the men were entangled in the nets, that were stated to have been met with about four miles from the shore.

A number of men rowed to the spot, and succeeded in lifting nearly four hundred fathoms of netting, beside ropes. This was towed near the shore awaiting the high tide, and later they landed it on the beach. The effluvia emitted led to the conjecture that the bodies of the men were enfolded within the meshes of the netting, and this turned out to be the case.

The stench however principally arose from the large quantities of decayed fish of many sorts which had been captured in the nets...WDM January 1877.

The Budleigh Salterton men had rowed many weary miles, towing behind them weighty fathoms of fishing nets. Fishermen near Mevagissey were curious about a large object they could see floating in the sea, and they in their turn set out to attempt to recover it.

MEVAGISSEY'S WHALE

A huge object floating in the sea a mile off Mevagissey was seen on Saturday morning, and a party of Gorran fishermen going out discovered it to be a dead whale. Fastening ropes to the fins of the huge fish, five boats commenced to tug away and after many weary hours succeeded in landing it on Colona beach about one mile from Mevagissey, where hundreds of eager spectators were awaiting the arrival of the monster which proved to be a rorqual or black whale of the following dimensions:- Length 61 feet, girth about 42 feet, spread of tail 14 feet, expansion of jaw about 15 feet. The lucky captors offered it for sale asking for their price £100, but ultimately sold it to a Mevagissey firm for £35.

The power of selling has since been questioned by the coastguard authorities who on telegraphing to their headquarters received orders to seize the prize, but did not do so until the fish was much shorn of its symmetry, as during the interim the purchasers had denuded it of the greater part of the blubber...WDM April 1875.

They did better out of their 'catch' than the men of Teignmouth. They too found a whale some distance offshore, but HM Coastguard intervened more quickly, and so their labours were in vain. Nevertheless it afforded considerable entertainment to the townsfolk.

WHALE TOWED TO TEIGNMOUTH

As some men were returning in a boat belonging to a man named Ellis on Monday evening from their day's labour on the whiting ground, they observed in the distance a large black object tossing about in the sea. They immediately bore down upon it. They at first thought that it was a portion of a wreck, but on nearing it discovered a large whale, it was dead, and they at once took it in tow. There was a fine breeze in their favour and they soon succeeded in getting a good way on their cumbersome prize. They at length reached the mouth of the harbour, but could not enter, and they accordingly moored their whale outside. By yesterday morning the whale had drifted on to the beach at New Cove, and as the tide fell it was left high and dry. It measured fifty feet in length, and was about thirty feet in girth, it was very fat and considered to be about twenty tons in weight. In the morning several fish buyers offered to purchase it, but the Coastguard gave instructions that no part of the fish was to be removed. The beach was crowded with people during the day, such a spectacle being of course a novelty. It is supposed that the whale had been dead for several days... WMN January 1875.

The beach was crowded with people, such a spectacle being a novelty.
Rosie Fierek.

It must have been the heaviest catch these fishermen had seen in years! Sometimes though, there were rare occasions when fishing brought rather different rewards than had been anticipated.

BRAVERY RECOGNISED

A short time ago the fishing lugger *Catherine* was on the fishing ground off Porthleven, and when in the act of preparing to shoot the nets a lad named Pascoe fell overboard without making any alarm. A youth named

W.H.Mathews heard the splash and saw Pascoe struggling in the water at some distance from the boat, for the boat was drifting fast before a fresh breeze.

He immediately sprang into the water to the rescue. The other two occupants then threw two oars to Mathews and seizing one of them he swam to the drowning lad who by this time was about to sink for the last time. Rousing him, he got him to rest on an oar until the lugger which was at once got under sail and worked up to windward took both rescuer and rescued aboard...A subscription list was started at Helston on Mathew's behalf which resulted in the sum of £5.18 shillings being collected.

An English lever watch and albert were purchased. They were presented to him by Mr J.Simmons harbourmaster at Porthleven, accompanied by suitable words of encouragement...WMN December 1875.

EIGHT

THE CAPTAINS

'Suitable words of encouragement', might have been made by the Harbourmaster at Porthleven - whether ships' captains were given to such a kindly approach is open to doubt. Ships are not usually commanded by a consensus of opinions, and the master's authority, be it a tiny fishing boat or a large full rigger was usually final.

Press accounts are always careful to give the dignity of office to the skipper, and the smallest smack will have her captain's name linked to her.

Compulsory standards of qualification had been laid down for Masters and Mates by the Mercantile Marine Act of 1850, and from 1883 for the Skippers and Mates of fishing vessels.

It was very hard work to obtain a certificate of competency. A skipper's ticket for a foreign going vessel required four years of sea-time as an apprentice. This was aboard a deepwater vessel trading outside home limits, and the four years sea-time meant just that. Any time ashore had to be made good in order to reach the four years.

The examination for the second mate's ticket could then be taken, and after that a minimum of two more years was required before sitting for a mate's qualification; if successful at least one more year was needed before attempting the skipper's ticket, and then there might well be years as a first officer, before the chance of command came along.

It is not surprising in view of the responsibility they carried, and of the isolation of command, that at times they come across as very obstinate or eccentric men.

Sometimes it was drink that got to them. The *Daylight* arrived in the Thames with news of a skipper using his gun.

CAPTAIN FIRES AT CREW

The *Daylight*, Captain Abrahmson, from Swan River has arrived in the Thames. The master reports that on February 3rd in latitude 3N longitude 25W he fell in with the *Ilva*, barque of Dundee, bound from Cadiz to Montivideo, cargo salt, flying a signal of distress. On boarding her it was ascertained from the mate (Pyatt), that on the previous day the master (Captain Clark), during a fit of drunkenness had shot at a boy, fired at the mate, and others of the crew. Upon the crew attempting to secure him, he had jumped overboard and was drowned. On Captain Abrahmson's advice all the spirits on board were thrown into the sea. The mate who held a master's certificate, stating that he felt capable of taking the vessel to Pernambuqo, and being satisfied with the behaviour of the crew, and there being no entrance of insubordination against the men in the log book - at noon the vessels parted company, and the *Ilva* when last seen was steering about SSW...WDM April 187

The drunken captain, in this next report, had rather better surroundings - his crew merely bundled him into his cabin and lashed the door shut.

Generally there are not too many reports on the south-west coasts which blame drink as a major factor. It was rather different off our eastern seaboard though, because it was there that the notorious 'grog' ships traded openly among the fishing fleets.

Captain Coye was in the minority then, he seems to have been determined to celebrate his New Year in some style. It might well be that by the gesture of throwing overboard his quadrant and chronometer he was anticipating the verdict of the court of inquiry! One can but sympathise with his long suffering first mate.

SKIPPER THROWS AWAY CHRONOMETER

The official inquiry into the circumstances attending the loss of the schooner *Fanny* in Tranmore Bay on the 3rd January has been held at Waterford...

On the last day George Vivian the boatswain deposed that the captain was under the influence of drink from the time they sailed from Cardiff on the 30th December until the time they sighted the Irish Coast on the 3rd January.

When first seen the mate thought that they were making for Waterford harbour, but having consulted his chart he told the captain that he was steering the vessel in on Brownstown Head, Tranmore Bay. The captain replied by saying that there was a harbour inside there somewhere, and he persisted in steering the vessel into Tranmore Bay.

By the time they were opposite Brownstown Head the captain was so drunk that the mate seeing that the vessel would become stranded got the chains and anchors in position but the captain prevented their use and said the vessel would not do herself any harm.

He at the same time ordered the jolly boat to be lowered, when it was fastened to the ship by a painter. The captain then threw his chronometer and quadrant overboard, and he himself got into the jolly boat but when he tried to cut her adrift he was prevented by the witness. He then got him on deck, but he persisted that the vessel should be allowed to drift into the breakers.

The crew ultimately had to lash him into his cabin...the court giving judgment suspended Captain Coye's certificate for three years...WDM February 1877.

Crews on the longer voyages could experience hardships caused by the behaviour of their skippers, and the skippers find frustrations with their crews. Very often these disputes ended up in court when the vessel made port, and their outome was not always predictable.

These were of course the days before auxiliary engines became commonplace, and a major anxiety for a skipper would be to find his vessel being blown on to a lee shore, with his sea room rapidly diminishing.

Incidentally, initial names for ships were not uncommon, sometimes they reflected the consortium which owned the boat, or sometimes they were the initials of the owner's name.

CAPTAIN KICKS SEAMAN IN FACE

At Stonehouse Petty Sessions yesterday John Bourne, captain of the barque *WLJ*, now lying in the Great Western Docks, was summonsed for assaulting George Axe, Mr R.J.Edmunds defended.

The prosecutor stated that he was a seaman aboard the *WLJ*, and that on the the afternoon of the 21st February, while the ship was at sea he was at the wheel, it was blowing a gale, and as the vessel pitched he was thrown from the helm upon the deck, whereupon the defendant came out of his cabin and struck him several times and kicked him in the mouth.

In answer to Mr Edmunds it was denied that he shipped on board the *WLJ* as an able seaman, but he received thirty-five shillings on joining the vessel. Mr Edmunds in defence stated that the complainant received

£3/15 shillings a month - able seaman's wages, but that he was utterly incompetent to perform an AB's duty. On the day in question the complainant was steering the vessel within six miles of a dead lee shore on the coast of France. The defendant discovering that the ship was endangered spoke to Axe about it, but that he was bound to admit that he the defendant did strike him, but he was provoked so to do.

The bench observed that the defendant was not justified in committing assault, although the complainant had provoked him by placing the ship in such a perilous position, and that therefore they would fine him the nominal sum of five shillings with costs...WMN March 1877

A Board of Trade inquiry at Plymouth in March 1877 gives an insight into the worries of skippers about their navigation when leaving the Bristol Channel, particularly if bound for Spain or Portugal.

Their courses would be such that if the winds turned foul they would have the Scilly Isles under their lee, plus the Longstones, and the Sevenstones reef.

Richard Dyer was skipper of the schooner *Ethel*, he was worried about the weather, and had stayed on deck for over thirty-six hours before finally turning in fully dressed for a cat nap. The *Ethel* struck the Sevenstones reef whilst he was asleep.

VESSEL STRIKES SEVENSTONES ROCKS

A Board of Trade inquiry was held in Plymouth Guildhall yesterday into the conduct of the master of the *Ethel*, a schooner of Plymouth 119 tons regular owned by Mr James King, in the navigation of his vessel when it struck the Sevenstones reef on the 17th February...

The *Ethel* left Newport on the 8th February the crew consisting of six hands all told. She had on board a cargo of 195 tons of coal bound to Cadiz. Meeting with contrary winds she put into Penarth Bay, and remained there until the 16th. On the morning of the 17th she was hove to under Lundy Island for three hours and a half. At half past seven she proceeded down channel...

At about eight o'clock that evening the *Ethel* was seventeen miles nor'west of Longships, and at ten she was about eight or nine miles from the Sevenstones and heading sou' by west. The mate was then in charge. At about a quarter before midnight she struck on the Sevenstones heavily, three times, and passing over continued her voyage.

Next day finding considerable damage was done the master brought the ship into Plymouth for repair.

Richard Dyer, master of the *Ethel*, deposed that he had a certificate of competence. The vessel drew ten feet six inches for'ard and twelve feet three aft. Her masts, sails, and stores were in good condition. There were two pumps, and a boat large enough to hold all the crew. Going down channel the wind was nor'nor west and squally, and he allowed half a point for the set of the swell to leeward. At eight o'clock on the evening of 17th February he was relieved by the mate, having been on deck for thirty-six hours since leaving Penarth Roads.

When the mate took charge the vessel was sixteen miles NNW of the Longships lighthouse, and was heading WSS, but he calculated that she was making WSW. The wind was from the NW moderate. He gave the mate instructions to call him if there was a difference in the wind or weather, or if the ship continued to break off. He then went below and laid down in his clothes.

At ten he was called by the mate who told him the

ship had broken off SW, going on deck he found this was true, and saw the Longships light SWS by W nine miles. Finding the ship could not possible weather the Scilly Isles, he determined to go between the Sevenstones and the Scilly. The distance being seven miles.

He gave directions to the mate to this effect saying if the ship continued to break off, or if there was any change in wind or weather he should be spoken to in time, and he would tack to the westward. They were then close hauled, and the course the ship was making then he calculated, would have taken them three or four miles off the Sevenstones and the western rocks.

He remained below until the ship struck about an hour and three quarters after at about a quarter to twelve. He rushed on deck saw his position and let go the peak of the mainsail, the lee forebraces, and backed the headyard and the vessel backed off and then passed along. He gave orders to try the pumps and little or no water was making, and not satisfied he ordered the pumps to be sounded, there were seven or eight inches .

They passed the Sevenstones light about midnight to the SW and close to. They proceeded on their way. The following morning he noticed a piece of copper was off the forefeet on both sides, but was making little water. They continued until about half past one when they bore up, after consulting the crew for Plymouth...WDM March 1877.

The *Ethel* had run for Plymouth in the winter of 1877, and a court there was also listening to the story of a French skipper who had refused to attempt such a trip, on grounds of severe weather. One suspects in fact, that he much preferred to spend Christmas at home, rather than at sea in the cold English Channel.

LEGAL ACTION OVER TARDY VOYAGE

In the Stonehouse County court yesterday before Mr Mathew Fortune - Judge, assisted by two nautical assessors. John Onley-Nash, potato merchant of Plymouth sued Captain Roulle of the sloop *Marie Francois*, for damage caused by unreasonable delay in bringing a cargo of potatoes from Parros to Plymouth .

It was stated that on or about the 15th December he had bought a cargo of potatoes and became indorsee of the bill of lading of the cargo of the defendants vessel. The vessel did not arrive in Plymouth until the 7th February, when the potatoes were found to be greatly injured by salt water, and by having germinated, and the price of potatoes had also fallen to thirteen shillings a ton.

Several witnesses were called to prove that vessels of the same size and rig had made the voyage from Parros and adjacent ports, to Plymouth quite successfully during the months of December and January. For the defendant it was contended that he had used every endeavour to complete the voyage in accordance with the terms of the charter party, but had been prevented by the tempestuous weather and circumstances over which he had no control.

He stated that on the 19th December he sailed from Parros but had to put back again on the 25th. He again sailed on the 9th January when he lost his mainsail and jib, and had to return, his mainsail was not ready until 3rd February, when he again put to sea - but had to return, but on the 5th he once more sailed and successfully reached Plymouth on the 6th. The judge and assessors after a long consultation gave verdict for the plaintiff for £28 ten shillings, this was £15 less than the amount claimed... WMN February 1877.

Richard Dyer of The *Ethel* had been prepared to consult with his crew before taking a decision to run for Plymouth. In some cases though crews were refractory, and more than willing to take matters into their own hands.

UNWILLING SEAMEN AT FALMOUTH

William Evans a seaman on board the three masted schooner *Jane Stewart* of St Johns, Newfoundland, yesterday sued Captain Neil Macdonald his master for four pounds for wages allegedly due.

The complainant stated that the *Jane Stewart* left Antwerp for St Johns with a cargo of bricks on the 9th September last, after being at sea for a few days she experienced heavy westerly gales causing several sails to split, and compelling the throwing overboard of nearly twelve thousand bricks. The decks were swept and the vessel was put back.

Mr Tilley on behalf of the master complained of the conduct of the crew including the chief officer. He said the vessel was within three days sail or 500 miles from the port of destination, but in consequence of the actions of the crew the captain was compelled to put back to Falmouth, a distance of 1,500 miles, just three times the distance from that port where they were bound.

The captain was willing to pay the complainant one pound and give him his discharge. The bench stopped the case and spoke of the conduct of the crew as being very reprehensible, making no order for the payment of wages...WMN October 1876.

Then there were the cases of runaway crews. In October 1876 the crew of a ship bound for Boston deserted en masse. They planned it quite well, even to the extent of smuggling their clothes ashore. In the end they were apprehended, but the skipper was forced to agree to their terms, and discharge the mate, the alleged cause of their discontent.

A RUNAWAY CREW

On Thursday morning at about 9.30 a.m the seven crew of the *Millie Bain* of Hayle, Captain Cook, bound from Fowey to Boston, America, took the ship's boat and rowed up to Fowey harbour. They deposited their clothes in the Cornwall mineral railway station, giving orders to have them sent on to Plymouth.

They then went in the ship's boat across to Bodenough, left the boat there and set off on the high road in the direction of Plymouth. Captain Cook was ashore transacting the ship's business, and had information given him as to what had happened. He immediately gave notice to PC Warren, went to the railway station and stopped the clothing from being sent on.

He then took a conveyance in company with PC's Warren and Spry, and arriving at Peakwater they found the men had passed there, and inquired their distance from Looe to which place they at once went. On arriving there the police found five of their number in a public house. They were at once taken in charge, and brought back to Fowey, and sent on to the police station at Tywardreath for the night. Yesterday they were brought before the magistrate and on being asked if they would return to their duty they consented and at once went on board. The two men who are still missing are William Hill and Philip Richards. It appears that all hands did not care about the mate of the vessel, and the captain has had to discharge him...WMN October 1876.

Attempts at desertion did not always end so happily. An inquest in Plymouth in September 1879 describes the end of one such attempt.

DEATH FROM DROWNING

An inquest was held at the Prince Rock Inn at Laira, by the Plymouth coroner last evening relative to the death of a German of about 22 years of age.

Herman Diederick Borrack, a German, mate of the *Orient*, brigantine of Balankenese, Germany, gave his evidence through an interpreter.

He stated that the *Orient* was lying in the Cattewater. The deceased was an ordinary seaman on board and at half past seven on Wednesday evening two men belonging to the *Orient* had left the ship in a passing boat to go ashore, just as the boat left the ship the deceased shouted to the men in the boat that he wanted to go. But witness who had charge of the deck at the time prevented him from going with the men as he had not permission to go ashore, and when the deceased shouted after the boat it did not return.

Deceased mounted the railings, but witness took hold of him by the sleeve to prevent him from going after them. The deceased had a belaying pin in his hand and raised it in a threatening manner and said "If you do not let me go I will knock you on the head", witness let go his arm in order to take away the belaying pin, and said "Do not jump overboard I'll get the revolver", then turned towards the cabin to get the revolver - but immediately turned round and saw the deceased in the act of springing from the railing of the vessel about amidships. The deceased tried to swim but could not.

Witness ran to the stern of the vessel and threw a lifebuoy just in front of him, but he believed the deceased was incapable of seeing it as he was insensible.

The boat at this time was about ten yards from the ship, he then saw the deceased splash his hands in the water and sink, and he never rose again. Not more than a minute elapsed from the time the deceased shouted to the other men in the boat until he jumped overboard and sank.

There was sufficient light at the time for the witness to see all of this, when the deceased sank the boat containing the two sailors from the ship was about twenty yards from the vessel... He thought the object of the deceased in jumping overboard was not to drown himself, but to go ashore in the boat containing the two other sailors in order that he might run from the ship.

He thought this because the deceased had his best clothes on at the time, because he the deceased was afraid of the punishment he would receive in Germany for stealing some clothes, and a watch and a chain belonging to the witness in St Nazaire in France. He had then ran away from the ship but had been caught and brought back.

The deceased had a very comfortable ship, and plenty to eat and drink. The captain of the vessel was in his cabin when the deceased jumped overboard, but he was called immediately and came on deck. The other two sailors who went away from the ship had permission to go ashore for the evening. The ship at the time of the occurrence was lying midstream about sixty yards from the shore...WMN September 1879.

There were times of course when physical attacks on the officers involved nothing short of full scale mutiny, and then firearms were needed. The skipper of the fishing boat *Secret* returned to Plymouth with news of a mutiny and murder aboard an American schooner.

MUTINY AND MURDER

Mr Chester master of the fishing boat *Secret*, of Worthing, at present engaged in the Plymouth fishery reports that he boarded an American three-masted schooner, *Jefferson Borton*, about 20 miles off the Eddystone and he was informed that a serious mutiny had occurred on that vessel. About ten days ago three of the crew - one a native of Russian Finland, another a Frenchman, and the third an American - mutinied and murdered the first mate whose body they threw overboard. Afterwards they seized and threw overboard the second mate, who was drowned, and then they attacked the captain, but he having armed himself with a revolver shot down the mutineers, one of whom he severely wounded, and the other two who were only slightly wounded were placed by him in irons. One man was chained to the pump.

The *Jefferson Borton*, which sails from Boston, was on a voyage from New Orleans with a general cargo, and when the *Secret* boarded her she was in company with a Norwegian barque, whose captain had placed some men aboard to assist navigate her to London. Previous to the barque rendering assistance the vessel was being worked by the captain (whose wife was aboard), and three hands. No reason was given for the mutiny, but Mr Chester expresses the opinion that there is not the slightest reason to doubt the accuracy of this report.

This vessel is what is sometimes termed a 'family' ship. The captain's wife was aboard - his brother

Croydon T. Patterson was first mate, and his cousin Chas
C. Patterson was the second mate aboard her...WMN
May 1875

This next report tells of a truly pig-headed captain, and of rescue
by breeches buoy. Such rescues become quite numerous from the
1860's onward. One reason for this was the reorganisation of the
Coastguard service in 1856.

It had been transferred from Customs to Admiralty control and
oversight, and its role had gradually enlarged from a coastwatch anti-
smuggling service, to one which also offered a life saving function.
This was via the many volunteer life saving companies it had helped
to train.

Sir William Congreve, later to become a Member of Parliament for
Plymouth, had perfected a rocket in the early 1800's which had a
range of 2,000 yards. This was designed, and at first used for military
purposes, but towards the middle of the 19th century was increasingly
employed for breeches buoy use, and it proved to be most effective
in this role.

Breeches buoys saved many lives, particularly in coastal areas
where high cliffs made it difficult to get easy access to stranded craft.

Captain Kergulant of Vannes ran his ship ashore in Mount's Bay,
but he seems to have been resolute in his determination to refuse all
aid from the shore - much to the exasperation of his would-be rescuers.

RELUCTANT RESCUE

On Saturday morning soon after ten o'clock a mounted
message arrived at Penzance Customs House with the
news that a brig, supposed to be French, was ashore at
Perran beach. Mr A.D Phillip the Deputy Receiver of
Wrecks, and Mr Edwin T.Mathews the French vice-consul
proceeded with all despatch to the spot.

The maritime rescue apparatus was at once got out and taken to Perran. At the time the wind was blowing strongly from the south with pretty much sea.

The rocket apparatus having arrived the coastguards fired several rockets over to the vessel, of which the crew took not the slightest notice. At length they hauled in the hawser, but apparently were in ignorance as to how to work it for they fastened the hawser on board and did not haul in the snatch block. One of the crew named Joseph however hauled himself ashore on the line. From the Mount, a barge belonging to Sir John St Aubyn, and manned by young fishermen put out and got alongside, but the crew refused to leave. From Penzance the rockets that were fired could be seen, it being thought that they could not reach the crew who were to be seen on board.

Mr John Mathews the local Hon Sec of the Royal National Lifeboat Institution, immediately gave orders for the *Richard Lewis* lifeboat to proceed, which she did under canvas. On her arrival alongside the crew took not the slightest notice, not even throwing a line, indeed they could not get the slightest assistance from the captain or the crew. The captain not being willing that the crew should leave.

The sea was gradually increasing, and the wind veering to the westward, the vessel being in the breakers full of water, and about five or six hundred yards from the shore. The lifeboat however stuck by the vessel a considerable time, and finally five of her crew got into her, leaving the captain quite alone on board. He positively refused to quit the vessel, and the lifeboat rowed off some distance, but however she returned to the wreck and urged the captain to come on board but he would not. There being no other recourse Coxswain Trewhella had finally to leave the vessel's side, hoping the captain might possibly be rescued with the aid of the rocket apparatus. During the time the lifeboat was alongside she was struck by several heavy seas which nearly swamped her, and had three oars broken.

The Penzance lifeboat rowing out to the Jeune Hortense. The lifeboat's carriage is in the foreground of the picture. Gibson, Isles of Scilly.

The five men were taken to Penzance harbour where they were landed, attention being paid to their requirements. Soon after the lifeboat left the wreck, Commissioned Boatswain Gould who was with the rocket apparatus volunteered to undertake the perilous duty of going out on the rocket line, with a view of urging the captain to save his life - taking with him a letter from

the vice-consul. Gould got into the breeches and commenced hauling himself off to the vessel. By this time
the vessel was evidently broken into two, as her masts
were yawing in different ways as the seas were sweeping her.

A most exciting scene ensued amidst a breaking and
heavy sea, Gould gradually drew himself out till he got
under the bows of the brig. The captain did not take
any more notice of Gould than he had of the lifeboat.
Gould got out of the breeches (having a lifebuoy on)
and endeavoured to swim up and get on board, but in
doing so the sweep of the seas broke over him with
such fury that he was washed off, and all on shore
dreaded that he was lost. On shore they slackened the
hawser hoping that Gould might get to it, this he fortunately managed to do, and finding he could do nothing
more he was hauled ashore in the most exhausted state.

Meanwhile the vessel was fast breaking up, first of all
the stern where the captain was standing carried away,
soon after the topsides of the vessel broke all away, the
masts fell over the side towards the shore and the captain who mounted to the rigging was hurled down and
buried in the debris. For some time it was feared he was
lost, but some minutes afterwards he was seen in the
wreckage, and finally got hold of the foreyard, the sail of
which rather sheltered him.

The coastguards now fired more rockets over the
wreck, the line of one of which the captain seized.
Owing to the quantity of floating wreckage he had the
greatest difficulty in getting into the breeches buoy from
where he was, as the line was continually fouled. Having
got hold of the breeches buoy he partly stripped himself,
got into it, and the men on shore hauled away. Several
heavy seas nearly overwhelmed the captain, and at one
time it was feared that he was gone, on nearing the

shore the coastguards ran out line in hand as far as they could get, and when the captain got within reach he was firmly grasped and a few moments saw him rescued and ashore.

Whilst this thrilling scene had been enacted Mr J. Mathews had telegraphed to the Penzance and the Porthleven lifeboats to come out at once, but he was able to intercept the Penzance boat when off the Mount. The foolhardy captain was at once taken care of, but he did not appear much exhausted. The vessel has broken up and is a total wreck. She proved to be the French brig *Ponthien*, 145 tons register, Captain Kergulant (said to be the principal owner) of Vannes, bound from Pomaron to Liverpool with iron pyrites. She had put into Mounts Bay for shelter, and on Saturday morning set sail, the wind having changed. She got embayed and driven ashore at Perran beach. The vessel appears to have got embayed owing to her mainyard having given way, so she could set no after canvas. Before she got ashore two anchors were let go, but their cables parted...WDM May 1879.

A rocket brigade was again called out when Captain Shannon mistook Portland Bill for Start Point, a mistake which many people have made in poor visibility.

His attempt to 'stay' his vessel was an effort to go about by bringing her bows through the direction of the wind, and this would have put her on the other tack and allowed her to sail clear. This having failed he next attempted to alter direction by 'wearing' ship, or presenting her stern to windward. This too was doomed; and his would-be rescuers once again had a frustrating time.

The result of 'missing stays'. The Lizzie R. Wilce (nearest the camera) stranded near St. Ives. Gibson, Isles of Scilly.

VESSEL ASHORE AT PRAWLE

At half-past three yesterday morning a watchman at Prawle Coastguard Station saw a vessel in a dangerous position, and he showed his blue light upon which those on board tried to 'stay', but there being a heavy sea the vessel refused, and struck on a reef of flat rocks some distance from the shore.

The rocket apparatus was got out under the direction of Mr G.Blackler the Chief Officer and an attempt was made to communicate with her, but before the line was got on board three rockets were fired, after getting the hawser off the crew of the imperilled vessel did not seem to know what should be done.

They appeared to have made fast the breaching line on board and under these circumstances it was a long time before they were all landed. They were five in number, and they belonged to the schooner *Utility* of Fleetwood, 90 tons register bound to Runcorn with a cargo of boulders and flintstone.

The master Captain Shannon stated that he left Shoreham on Sunday last and had encountered very bad weather in the Channel. On Thursday he was off the Bill at Portland, and judging from his patent log he thought at the time of the occurrence that he was in the neighbourhood of the Start. The weather was being too thick for him to see the light of that place, the wind which had been blowing from the south fell in the night and got around to sou'sou'west, and was blowing a fresh gale, when at about half past three o'clock land was observed through the fog and he attempted to 'stay', but this was unsuccessful and he then tried to wear. The *Utility* is full of water and with a southerly wind will probably soon break up. With regard to the crews' ignorance of the manner of working the rocket lines it is to be regretted that the owners do not more generally accept the offer of the Board of Trade to supply free of charge enamel plates containing instructions as to their use...WDM October 1877.

There are numerous accounts of the use of the rocket apparatus around the coasts of the south west of England. One records an incident at Padstow in March 1876, and reads as if it is dismissive of the fact that one man was drowned - on the grounds that he was only a foreigner!

Padstow was a notoriously difficult port to enter without local knowledge because of its infamous Doom Bar. The name in fact is a corruption of 'dune or dun', and nearly three hundred boats were wrecked on this shifting sandbar within one hundred and fifty years.

PADSTOW SHIPWRECK

On Tuesday evening the cry was up that a vessel, apparently disabled, was running for the harbour. The tide being ebb and a very heavy sea it caused considerable excitement amongst the maritime inhabitants.

The shipwrights' gigs were speedily manned and proceeded to Stepper Point in waiting. The steam tug *Amazon* followed, and the *Albert Edward* lifeboat got in readiness.

Between eight and nine o'clock the vessel came up off the harbour but having no after canvas on her could not get in. She drifted across to Hell Bay. The lifeboat went after her but could not get near her for the heavy sea.

Finally she went ashore on Trebetherick Rocks, St Miniver. The Rocket Brigade was successful in getting their apparatus aboard by which the captain and five of the crew were landed. One man a foreigner, fell out of the basket and was drowned...WMN March 1876.

The rocket apparatus was not the only method of rescue at Padstow - sometimes it was the lifeboat which did sterling work, even to the extent of rescuing the ship's pets!

ABANDONED VESSEL AT PADSTOW

At about two o'clock this afternoon the Italian brigantine *Immaculate*, of Naples, Leonardo Marielle master bound from Corfu with a cargo of bones for Falmouth, for orders, tried to enter Padstow harbour while the wind which was accompanied by rain was blowing a strong gale from the southwest. In making the attempt however she missed stays, and shortly afterwards brought to anchor in a dangerous proximity to the Doom Bar.

The *Albert Edward* lifeboat, belonging to the Royal National Lifeboat Institution was launched at 4.30 from Hawkes Cove, and under the command of Coxswain Digory Crowthers proceeded to the vessel and took off and brought ashore the crew consisting of the captain, his son, five men and a boy. The captain saved the ship's papers, and some of the crew brought away a portion of their clothes and two dogs. The gale is violently increasing, and should the wind shift to the NW the vessel will go to pieces... WMN 1875.

There were times of course when the problems at Padstow were in the immediate vicinity of the port. The steam tug *Amazon*, active in one of the previous reports was again involved.

KETCH SINKS UNDER TOW

On Friday afternoon the ketch *Anna Louisa* of Chepstow, Charles Wheatstone, master, from Lydney to Padstow with coals went ashore in Perran Bay nearer to the west of Newquay, having mistaken it for the entrance of Padstow harbour. The vessel grounded on a flat beach and by means of discharging cargo etc she was got off on Monday.

The steam tug *Amazon* of Padstow was telegraphed for, and about six o'clock in the evening it began to tow the *Anna Louisa* toward Padstow. Aboard the ketch were her crew of four men, and four others belonging to Perran who went to assist in pumping. All went well until half-past nine o'clock when the vessels were just abreast of Trevose Head lighthouse. The wind was blowing strongly from the westward and there was an ebb tide running down at about eight knots an hour causing a deal of sea.

About this time those on board the steamer heard shrieks from the ketch which was 45 fathoms astern.

Her sails in tatters the Olympe lies abandoned near Mullion. A human 'chain' of rescuers waded into the surf to take off her crew when she ran aground in 1910.

The cries were that she was sinking, the *Amazon* was quickly backed astern but the vessel suddenly lurched to starboard and foundered bow foremost, it was with difficulty that the tow rope was cast off from the steamer, and fortunately so, or a more fatal calamity would probably occurred. Lines from the steamer were thrown to the struggling men, four of whom were thus hauled on board. Two others who had supported themselves on the wreckage were next rescued, but not until one had been in the water for half an hour. The other two poor fellows had sank soon after the foundering of the vessel. They were one of the crew named Oliver Morgan aged 21 belonging to Bridgwater, and Thomas Glasson of Perran aged 23 years... WMN August 1879

Language often proved a barrier when it was foreign boats in difficulties. Six months later another French boat went aground. This time it was at Torcross on the south coast, and again the coastguard were on hand with their rocket gear. The rescuers found it difficult to discover anything about the crew, or the crew their rescuers - 'mundic' was the Cornish name for pyrites.

FRENCH BRIG ASHORE AT TORCROSS

During the gale on Saturday afternoon a brig was observed by the coastguards to be in distress off Torcross, as the wind was blowing a gale from the east it was evident by those able to judge that the brig must soon run ashore. Accordingly the coastguard got ready in all haste to prepare for the catastrophe. In a short time the vessel was on the sands. The coastguardmen succeeded in saving by their rocket apparatus all hands, seven in number.

The brig was laden with mundic and is now a total wreck, and no part of the cargo could be saved. In so much as not a single person at Torcross could speak French, no particulars could be learned from the survivors all of whom were totally ignorant of English...WDM Nov 1878.

The crew of the French schooner *Amiable* found themselves in a similar position when her skipper ran her ashore in the Penarth Roads. This time however there was no lifesaving brigade on hand, and judging by the phrasing of the press reports the crew were quite insistent that their skipper must abandon ship without delay. He went along with their decision, but the final outcome was not a happy one.

FATAL WRECK IN BRISTOL CHANNEL

Early this morning the French schooner *Amiable*, Baron master and laden from Cardiff to Nantes was totally wrecked on Cardiff Sands, Penarth Roads. The schooner left Cardiff on Saturday afternoon and and had reached a little below the Mumbles Head on Sunday afternoon, when owing to bad weather she had to put back.

She arrived in Penarth Roads shortly before midnight, the wind blowing very heavily and the night being very dark. The captain mistook the outer for the inner roads and was carried on to the sands.

The crew compelled the captain to leave in the boat but the frail craft shortly afterwards capsized. The men succeeded in righting the boat, and the captain, a seaman, and the boy got in. Three men tried to swim ashore but were not seen afterwards, and the boy died from exposure at four o'clock. The captain and the seaman were rescued two hours afterwards by the Dutch barque *Sandberg* eastward bound to Japan which was lying at anchor in the roads... WMN October 1875

The ship's boat was described in the previous account as "a frail craft", in fact they were usually clinker built, heavy and very stable.

It was used as maid of all work, and in these days before outboard engines was sculled, rowed or sometimes sailed. In harbour it would be made fast astern, and during short passages would be towed, rather than hoisted inboard. One of the easiest mistakes was to fail to make fast the painter of this tender - sometimes as the Western Morning News reported in August 1877, with near disastrous results.

THE SCHOONER MESSAGE OF DARTMOUTH

The schooner *Message* of Dartmouth came into Torbay on Sunday and in the evening the captain and two of his crew came ashore. They returned at 11 p.m, and on getting inboard they forgot to take in the boat's bow rope, and she soon drifted away. The other boat was got out, and two men jumped into her, in their excitement they forgot to take rowlocks. They were not able to pull and were driven out of the bay by the violence of the gale. They were however luckily picked up yesterday morning by a pilot cutter of Falmouth and were landed at Teignmouth, whence they returned to Brixham not much the worse for their cruise...WMN August 1877.

A simple error in failing to tie a knot properly had endangered the lives of the two crewmen, and they had been lucky to escape with nothing worse than a night spent tossing about uncomfortably at sea.

William Putt was an experienced skipper out for a day's fishing.

He seems to have erred in the opposite direction - and tied fast his main sheet which lead to his mainsail. It was done in such a fashion that when the sail filled with wind and the boat heeled over, he was unable to release it in a hurry. This had dire consequences.

FATALITY OFF SALCOMBE

Mr William Putt who has commanded several vessels in the coastal trade left his home at Salcombe yesterday to go fishing. He was returning with sail set and the sheet made fast when a puff of wind which was blowing in squalls caught the sail and upset the boat. Some men who saw the occurrence put off to the assistance of Mr Putt but could find nothing of him or of the boat. Captain Osborne and his son who were passing in a boat were told what had happened and after searching for some time they found the sprit of the boat which had sunk appearing above the water, and Mr Putt's body was found in the stern. The body did not appear to be entangled as it came up very freely when touched. Life was of course extinct, three quarters of an hour having elapsed from the sinking of the boat to its discovery...
WMN September 1875

Captain Thomas on the other hand was thousands of miles away when he died. He was in Peru; but it was determined to bring him back for burial in his native land - buried in the cargo of bird excrement! The West Briton reported his last journey.

BURIED IN GUANO

The *Northumbria*, from Peru with guano, arrived at

Falmouth on the 28th, having on board the body of the late respected master and part owner, Captain James Thomas, who died before the vessel sailed for England. The body was placed in a coffin there, packed with guano, and buried three feet deep in the cargo. On examination at Falmouth the corpse was found to be firm and in a perfect state of preservation. It was removed to St.Ives, and interred on Sunday morning...WB April 1873.

NINE

KILLER DISEASE

In addition to the hazards of weather, collision and accident, deep sea sailors faced another life threatening danger. This was scurvy, and many men sailing on the long voyages out of our deep water ports suffered from it. Falmouth, because of its position in our western approaches, saw numerous ships limping in with their crews disabled by this condition.

This is surprising in view of the fact the Scottish naval surgeon James Lind had showed in 1753, that it was a disease caused by dietary deficiency. It could easily be prevented by taking small quantities of lime, lemon or orange juices.

Captain Cook had followed this advice, and been awarded the Royal Society's 'Copley Medal' for his work in preventing scurvey among his crew. This was on his second long voyage of discovery in 1772-1775. He had insisted that their diet include cress, sauerkraut, and an extract of orange. In addition he had laid great stress on a high standard of cleanliness in the forecastle. Not one of his seamen had died from the disease.

Newspapers of the 1870's were still reporting numerous cases however, and appeared to be uncertain as to whether vitamin C deficiency really was the major cause. A writer to the Navy and Army Illustrated Magazine aired his doubts on the matter.

Opinions differ as to the value of limejuice as an anti scorbutic. It will be remembered that limejuice was not used on the last Arctic expedition. The Americans do not use it in their navy, preferring to rely on molasses, coffee and cheese. The term "limejuicer" is used as an expression of contumely by American sailors against our seamen. Most people consider limejuice a mawkish drink, so much so that captains who value the health of their men mix sherry with limejuice to ensure it being consumed...Navy and Army Magazine, February 1899.

Scurvy takes from upwards of two to six months to manifest itself. It begins with lassitude and loss of weight, and moves on to haemorrhage, ulcers of the mouth and gums, pains in the joints and muscles, severe anaemia and finally death.

The first of the following cases was in February 1876, and the ship in question, the *Royal Sovereign*, was reputed to be owned by one of the Members of Parliament for Plymouth - Mr Bates.

LIVERPOOL SCURVY SHIP PUTS INTO FALMOUTH

Several bad cases of scurvy are reported at Falmouth aboard the ship *Royal Sovereign* of Liverpool, 1,888 tons register. It seems that the ship the property of Mr Bates, MP for Plymouth sailed from Liverpool about thirteen months ago for Karachi via Bombay with a general cargo, under the command of Captain Neilson; before starting the trip, provisions were obtained from the owner's stores this included a quantity of salt beef and pork, concerning both of which there was a general complaint within three days after the vessel sailed on the voyage.

Indeed one of the men went aft to the captain with a plate of meat in his hand and stated the grievance, no notice however was taken of the matter, only a reprimand that he must not come again to the quarter deck with meat or anything else...

At Bombay a fresh supply of salt provisions was obtained, this was also of a very bad character, the pork was sour and rank and the beef putrid and not fit to be used. The men said that the only alternative left to them with such beef was to eat the wretched pork.

Captain Neilson died at Bombay, and the command fell to Captain Sumton, who was superseded at Karachi by Captain Drakeford.

The sugar and coffee were expended before the ship arrived at Karachi, and no preserved meat was issued during the voyage. The biscuit was also bad. From Karachi the ship sailed homewards bound for London, with a cargo of rapeseed, but yesterday she was obliged to put into Falmouth because of the sickness of eighteen of the crew, and their inability to work the vessel.

On arrival the ship was visited by Doctor Bullmore the port sanitary medical officer, who after examining the crew ordered them to be sent to the Sailors' Home, this was done. Those who suffered most actually being carried away on stretchers, only two able and two ordinary seamen are left fit for duty. All the men are very indignant and a Board of Trade inquiry is to be anticipated. The vessel will proceed to her destination if sufficient runners are available...WMN February 1876.

(Runners were casual seamen hired to work boats around the coast.)

Sailors were becoming readier to voice their complaints to the authorities ashore - though many of the reports seem to suggest that magistrates took a lot of convincing that ships' masters could ever be to blame.

FAILING TO SUPPLY LIMEJUICE

John Jones master of the British barque *Garfield* was charged with neglecting to supply limejuice to his crew in compliance with the Merchant Shipping Act. He was also charged under section 27 of the Act of 1863, with neglecting to carry, for certain periods sidelights.

Ernest Jones the mate of the above vessel was also charged with being asleep whilst on watch.

Alfred Carr stated that he had been an AB on board the *Garfield* of Glasgow, and shipped out of Galveston on 13th September, arriving in Plymouth Sound on the 26th November.

He asked the steward for some limejuice but he said there was none. When about a few weeks from Galveston they ceased to carry sidelights in the Western Ocean, this was owing to the paraffin having run short, and coal oil was used for substitute. For several times the lights were not lit, and in the Bay of Biscay the captain got some paraffin from a German brig. This lasted until they reached Plymouth.

Cross examined by Mr Stanbury the witness said that green pea soup without any meat in was served during the voyage. Witness was the worse for liquor when he complained at the Mercantile Shipping Office. Robert William corroborated, stating he had been in the mate's watch and on several occasions the mate was asleep when he was on duty - sometimes for an hour and sometimes more, he was also asleep on one or more occasions when the ship was in a dangerous spot...

Cross examined by Mr Stanbury: The mate had never pulled him out of the fo'castle when he ought to have been on watch. They had plenty of vinegar to drink as a substitute for limejuice, and plenty of preserved potatoes... John Jones captain of the *Garfield* stated he had been captain of the ship for about three years, the mate's general conduct had been quite satisfactory to him, the men were of a very indifferent character...the Chairman of the Bench after a few minutes stated that they could not find the case proved against the mate or the captain as regards the lights - but he thought there was some negligence on the part of the captain as regards the lime-juice, and must therefore inflict a penalty of five pounds and costs...WDM December 1878.

The German brig *Colibri* also had trouble with scurvy - the brief account throws an interesting sidelight onto a particularly unsavoury cargo. There would have been no mechanical aids to loading and unloading, and the stench must have been well nigh unendurable.

SCUTTLING OF GERMAN BRIG

The German brig *Colibri* from Australia bound for London which put into Falmouth on Friday last with her cargo on fire, was this morning towed into the beach near the town, and further efforts were made by pumping water into her hold to extinguish the fire, but without success. It was found necessary to scuttle her - this was done in the afternoon. She is now full of water. The cargo was a valuable one of manure, composed of smashed carcasses, bones, flesh, horns, hoofs, and entrails of cattle. The vessel left Kepple Bay on December 30th. The mate and steward have been sent to the Sailors' Home suffering from scurvy, and they allege that the vessel was short of provisions and that many of those on board were bad...WMN June 1878.

The Board of Trade were determined to stamp out the disease, and were anxious to investigate any reported cases of scurvy aboard British vessels. The Western Islands referred to in the text were the Scilly Isles.

STRICKEN SHIP IN FALMOUTH.

By direction of the Board of Trade Dr A.B.Harries the medical inspector of seamen and Mr R.B.Cheesman have held an investigation into the cause of the outbreak of scurvy on board the barque *Abercaren* of Glasgow.

The inquiry commenced on Wednesday...an examination of the vessel showed that the forecastle was close, and that at sea in rough weather water leaked into it. The beef and pork were good and not complained of by the men, other provisions were short, and sometimes half rations of rice and peas were served out. No flour had been issued to the crew for a month before arrival at Falmouth, and what was used before then was bad.

When passing the Western Islands, Lloyd the carpenter who has since died was very ill, the master on being asked to put into one of them for water and provisions declined to do so. He also refused to comply with suggestions from the crew that he get a supply from passing vessels.

The result of the inquiry as far as the conditions of the crew, shows that in addition to the death of Lloyd from scurvy and the four men brought on shore to the hospital suffering from the disease, all others including the captain are slightly affected ...WMN July 1878.

News of the the carpenter's death had spread, and an unruly mob was awaiting the skipper on his arrival at his home town of Swansea.

They shouted that he had starved his crew in order to line his own pockets, and the police arrived in the nick of time to rescue him from a severe beating up at the hands of the angry crowd.

THE BARQUE *ABERCARN*

Captain Lewis of the barque *Abercarn* just arrived at Swansea was mobbed by a number of people who declared that he had ill-treated and starved his crew. The police however interfered, and by dodging through several side streets the captain managed to get into a cab and was driven to the railway station for Aberdare. The ship is owned by Mr J.D.Jones, and during her voyage from Rangoon to Hamburg the crew were stricken with scurvy, and the carpenter a Swansea man died. This it is alleged was through the captain withdrawing the pre-scribed remedies in such cases. The crew were dis-charged at Falmouth and a Board of Trade Inquiry will now be held...WMN August 1878.

Even then, as late as 1878, not everyone was convinced about the causes of the disease. Newspapers were ready to blame over-crowding and a suspect water supply. This was at Falmouth again, the first major deepwater port in the south west approaches

PILOTS WORK VESSEL INTO HARBOUR

A large Danish fully rigged ship the *Freja*, Captain Hans Neilson arrived at Falmouth from Java on Sunday night. When boarded off the port by the Trinity pilot it was found that all the crew were more or less stricken with scurvy, and the pilot's men had to assist in working the ship into the harbour.

The vessel left Cardiff on the outward voyage on the 24th September 1877 for Singapore, and occupied 152 days in reaching there, by which time some of the crew were suffering from the disease.

She remained at Singapore fourteen days, and then after staying a month at Benoge, left for Falmouth. Her homeward journey took 129 days. The crew numbered 25 all told, all of whom are as we have stated more or less sick.

Fourteen are badly affected and the others are only just able to crawl about. There was a plentiful supply of water and provisions on board, and it is a mystery under these circumstances how so many men were struck down in the manner these are, excepting to the cause might be attributed the overcrowded state of the forecastle, also that for a short time rainwater was used instead of that in the tanks for drinking purposes.

The fourteen worst cases were brought ashore to the Sailors' Home, and their condition is truly pitiful...it is quite certain that had the voyage been more protracted some of them must have died...WDM August 1878.

TEN

CHANGING TIMES

Things though were slowly changing. The Merchant Shipping Act of 1876 had specified the load limits for cargo shipping. It required a series of lines, commonly known as Plimsoll lines after the MP Samuel Plimsoll who had sponsored the bill; to be painted on the hulls of British cargo ships. These showed the depths to which ships could be loaded safely.

This move went a long way towards helping to eliminate the so called 'coffin ships'. Many of these structurally unsound vessels, ill-found, undermanned and overinsured had been sent to sea by their greedy owners.

However there were still plenty of ships sailing under the British flag which were unsafe.

AN UNSEAWORTHY SHIP AT PLYMOUTH

At the Stonehouse Police Court yesterday the crew of the ship *Sunbeam* now lying in Plymouth Sound were charged on remand from Monday by the Master, Captain J.Dalmil with refusing to go to sea...

Captain John Stolt RN one of the Board of Trade Surveyors handed in a report which was read by the magistrate's clerk:- "The jibboom is rotten, the plank under the port cathead is rotten, and the calking bad; and the bits for the mainstays and maintopmast stays on the port side are completely gone to the great danger of the mainmast; the deckhouse for the crew is in bad condition; the mizzenmast has been properly tongued but not being wedged in the 'partners' is very unsafe; the calking around the starboard bow is bad, the running rigging is bad and there is only a small quantity of spars and rope on board; the sails are old and require overhauling, the boats are badly found.

I did not proceed with the survey as with these defects the ship is unfit to proceed to sea..."...WMN August 1875.

There was trouble in Brixham when five seamen refused duty aboard their vessel. They claimed that she was unsafe - and since *Truelove*, the boat in question was over a hundred and thirteen years old, their concern might have been justified.

DISOBEDIENT SEAMEN REFUSE 18TH CENTURY BOAT

At the Churston Ferrers courtroom on Saturday the five seamen charged with refusing to do duty on board the barque *Truelove* lying in Brixham Roads were again brought before the magistrates.

Truelove is one hundred and thirteen years old, having been built in Philadelphia in 1764 for the Greenland fisheries. She has changed hands two and three times in the last few years, and is at present owned by a London firm. She sailed sometime since with a cargo of coals for Tarragona, but sprung a leak which it appeared necessitated her putting back to Falmouth, and from this port she proceeded to Brixham to undergo certain repairs which were deemed necessary. While these repairs were being carried out the crew refused to work on board. They were brought back before the Justices last week and the Bench determined to call on the services of one of the Board of Trade Surveyors. Accordingly on Saturday morning Mr Shrigley, shipwright and surveyor visited the vessel, inspected her, and saw that the repairs were being affected...WDM Sept 1877.

By the latter half of the 1870's then, laws designed for the welfare of our seamen were slowly finding their way on to the statute book - and rather more importantly, were slowly beginning to be enforced; although it took some time for captains to appreciate this.

Captain Richard Ermington had packed his crew's quarters with stores, no doubt expecting that they would put up with 'hot bunking'. This was so called because two men shared a bunk, and the man coming off watch climbed into a bunk still warm from his predecessor's body. Captain Ermington was taken to court, found guilty and fined!

"I CAN DO WHAT I LIKE" SAYS CAPTAIN

At Stonehouse Police Court, yesterday, Richard Ermington captain of the barque *Hawke*, was summonsed by A. Johnston and A. Adams, two seamen of the above ship, for having between the 31st January and 16th July kept stores in the place allotted for and used by the seamen of the ship.

The ship had left for the Mediterranean on the 28th January, shortly afterwards the Captain had placed a quantity of sails and other stores in the berths of the crew. The crew consisted of four able seamen, two ordinary seamen, and a boy. They occupied eight berths in the forecastle. These stores having been placed on four of the berths though the crew were made to sleep on the other four.

Complaint was made to the Captain but he said that as long as he was master of the ship he could do as he liked. The evidence of the complainants was corroborated by Walter Taylor the mate of the vessel. The Captain was fined one shilling per head for each of the men for every day the stores had occupied their berths...WMN July 1876

Many seamen owed their lives to the rocket apparatus, as in this 1911 picture of the Hansey. Her crew were taken off safely by breeches buoy when she struck near the Lizard. Gibson, Isles of Scilly.

The regular Board of Trade Surveys, legislation to stop overloading, an efficient coastguard and lifeboat service, and established navigation marks did much for seafarers; and by the mid 1880's times were changing for the better.

Weather forecasting was beginning to be regarded as a more serious science - an embryonic Meteorological service had been set up in 1854. One of its early acts had been to provide reliable instruments on loan to skippers of deep water vessels, providing that they returned the instruments together with a log of their readings at the end of the voyage.

There was little that could be done of course about the steady attrition caused by the very natures of the job and the equipment. In October 1878 for instance the *Rippling Wave* of Fowey put into her home port with the sad news that her skipper had been washed overboard and lost.

CAPTAIN WASHED OVERBOARD

The *Rippling Wave* of Fowey from Brindisi for Hull with oil, put in here yesterday morning (i.e Fowey) with the loss of the master Captain Roberts of Polruan. The mate Mr William Toms reports that when in latitude 43 48N 4210 11W, they experienced a very heavy gale from the northwest, with heavy cross seas and the ship labouring heavily. At half-past four in the morning she shipped a sea over the weather quarter that washed Captain Roberts overboard, they threw the ladder and spars overboard, put the helm down and backed the topsail. Soon after the vessel shipped another sea which filled her, they could not manage the boat in such weather but they kept the vessel lying to until seven o'clock, they did not see anything of the captain and in consequence proceeded on the voyage home. The deceased was part owner of the vessel...WDM October 1878.

Or five fairly routine examples from the year 1876/1877:

An inquest was held at the Sailors' home on Saturday by the County Coroner respecting the death of Joseph Harries aged 29 years who had been a sailor on board the *Archibelle* from Gibralter during the gale on Wednesday last. The vessel was off the Scilly Isles when the deceased was struck on the head by the foreyard which bruised and stunned him besides inflicting some serious wounds. The captain put back to Falmouth to obtain medical aid, and the deceased was visited by Doctor Bullmore who thought it would be prudent to have him cared for in the Sailors' Home, but he died almost immediately on his arrival in that institution.

A man named Ceschi Luigi who has come from Cardiff and gone on board the *Fortune*, the ship from which four men were landed with the scurvy and are in Falmouth Sailors' Home, has been brought to the same institution with a broken leg. The accident having occurred when a chain cable caught him round the leg while at work. A man named Joseph Mitchell from the German barque *Strasbourg* has also been brought to the sailors' home with a broken arm. There are now four men lying at this institution with broken limbs. This Sailors' Home at Falmouth supplies the place of a hospital for seamen and deserves to be well supported by all the masters and vessels as well as by inhabitants.

A serious accident happened on Saturday morning to a young man named William Sanders on board the fishing boat *Merry Lass* of Brixham. The crew numbering four were engaged in heaving the trawl up with the winch when by some means the tackling became entangled, this necessitated the palls being lifted. On doing this the winch flew back at a tremendous rate, one of the handles striking Sanders on the head. His skull was laid open in two places for four inches in length. He remained insensible until taken ashore. He was attended by Mr G.Searl surgeon, under whom he is progressing favourably.

On Friday the fishing lugger *Nellie* left Porthleven for Mullion as a tender on the seine there. During the day one of the crew named John Laity, a young man of about twenty-one, took up a loaded gun with the intention of shooting a seagull. It suddenly discharged owing to the trigger coming into contact with something. Laity took up the gun by the barrel, the muzzle pointing towards his face. The consequence was that the charge struck the side of his face mangling it considerably, medical aid was secured and the wound dressed. The sufferer was brought home in the evening in a cab. It is hoped that he will progress favourably, although he is in danger of losing the sight of one eye.

A shocking accident occurred in Plymouth during Saturday night whereby two young men lost their lives, and a third has narrowly escaped death by suffocation.

It appears that a day or two since the South Devon Shipping Company's schooner *Leader*, Captain Dan, arrived at Plymouth and was berthed at her usual place alongside the South Devon wharf on the parade.

The whole of her cargo was discharged by Saturday afternoon. Then in consequence of rats having been seen below it was determined to smoke her in order to destroy the vermin, accordingly at five o'clock in the evening three pans filled with charcoal and pepper were placed, one in the cabin, one in the hold, and the third in the fo'c'sle and the contents were lighted. The entrance to the cabin was locked and the skylight closed, the hatches battened down and carefully secured. This having been done the whole of the apertures were covered with sails and tied down to avoid the possibility of any fumes escaping...shortly after 11 p.m three men were seen to go on board but no notice was taken of this by the person who saw it...

Yesterday morning a man went to the *Leader* to look for the men, and on going on board it was seen that an attempt had been made to gain admission to the cabin. The man went into the fo'c'sle where a terrible sight presented itself. Stretched on the floor were three men to all appearances lifeless. Two were lying on their backs, stiff cold and dead, in the middle of the compartment. The last was lying at the foot of the ladder where fortunately there was more air. He was found to be still alive but speechless. The three were taken out with the greatest expedition and taken to South Devon Hospital, but it was of no service to the two and they were taken to the dead house, the last one was taken in and restoratives were applied which proved successful in resuscitating him and he is now progressing favourably...WMN May 1877

It was undoubtedly a harsh way in which to earn a living, and for Thomas Ellis of Hayle the pressures mounted until they became unendurable, and his shipmates believed that he chose suicide as a way out.

He had been on watch on a previous trip when a collision had occurred and a man had drowned. This preyed on his mind, and the best efforts of his friends to cheer him up were of no avail. Nowadays he might have been diagnosed as clinically depressed.

SUICIDE AT SEA

A telegram from Captain Thomas Rogers of the schooner *Bessie* of Fowey stating that one of his crew named Thomas Ellis of Hayle was missing, was received at Hayle on Saturday.

The vessel on her last voyage to Plymouth ran down a fishing boat and a man was drowned. Ellis was one of the watch at the time, and it is supposed that the occurrence preyed on his mind as he had been in a despondent state for some time. On Friday when the Bessie bound for Neath was off the Lizard, Ellis was engaged in finding the jib, and afterwards went below and took off his boots. Shortly afterwards as the weather was very threatening the cook was sent forward to call the men to shorten sail. Ellis could not be found. It is supposed that he had jumped overboard as he had threatened to do so, he leaves a wife and five children...WMN July 1879

Not all the happenings were as dramatic as these, or involved boats on long journeys. John Cox and his son were merely delivering furniture when they ran into problems.

TEIGNMOUTH - BOATMAN AND BOY IN PERIL

On Saturday morning John Cox a boatman with his son left Teignmouth in in a large sailing boat for the purpose of conveying some furniture to Lyme. After unloading the boat they started homeward. The weather had changed, the wind having set in SE and there was a heavy swell on the bar. When Cox found the sea so rough he did not like attempting to run into the harbour. Consequently he brought up outside to wait until the tide flowed.

The wind and sea increased and he made up his mind to venture forward. In doing so the boat struck the bar and the sea broke over her. Both man and boy attempted to bale out the water but it was impossible to keep the boat free. Cox then launched the punt but a sea capsized her and she drifted away...Cox knowing the tide was low jumped overboard and found the water not very deep. He and the boy walked along the bank through the surf until they could go no further, when his son a lad of fifteen divested himself of as much clothing as he could swim ashore with and managed to reach land. A large boat was launched and Cox rescued from his perilous position just as breakers were threatening to wash him off the bank.

The lifeboat was got out but was not needed. There was of course the usual obstruction in the way of the lifeboat carriage lying on the beach, and until someone is drowned it will not be known who is responsible for keeping a clear passage in order that the boat shall be launched as quickly as possible... WMN November 1875

It seems fitting to me to end these accounts with mention of attempted rescues by lifeboat. The Royal National Institution for the Preservation of Life from Shipwreck, was founded in 1824, and evolved into the Royal National Lifeboat Institution in the early 1850's.

Volunteers who made up the lifeboats' crews placed their lives at risk, sometimes with tragic results. Cash incentives were not sought for, though token rewards were paid to the crews.

There are five different types of craft mentioned in the report, and of course they were the maids of all work of this period - barques, brigantines, schooners, sloops, and smacks.

ROYAL NATIONAL LIFEBOAT INSTITUTION

Yesterday a meeting of this institution was held at its house, John Street, London.

The secretary having read the minutes of the previous meeting, the Third Services Clasp of the Institution, and £3 were voted to James White, Coxswain of the Fishguard lifeboats, and £29 to the crew of these boats in acknowledgment of their recent gallant services in going out in a stormy gale and heavy seas and bringing safely ashore the crews numbering altogether twenty men, of the sloop *Adventure* of Bridgwater, the brigantine *B.Nash* of New York, the smack *George Evans* of Newquay, and the schooner *Supply* of Newport.

Rewards amounting to £214 were also granted to crews of other lifeboats of the Society for their services rendered during the past month.

The Padstow lifeboat saved the crew of the brigantine *Jeune Prospect*, and four men from the schooner *Plymouth* of Plymouth; which vessels were wrecked while trying to make Padstow harbour in a strong gale from N.N.W and a heavy sea. The Port Isaac lifeboat brought ashore four of the crew of the barque *Ida Melmore* of Maryport, that vessel being in a perilous position on a rocky lee shore...WDM March 1877.

The Bude boat was lost in the same month:-

LIFEBOAT CAPSIZED AND COXSWAIN DROWNED

The night of the wreck was exceeding dark, and the lifeboat *Elizabeth Moore* was taken from her station at 9.15 by a crew of twelve men, all had their cork lifejackets supplied to them, and   with a hearty endeavour the lifeboatmen were determined if possible to reach the wreck and render assistance.

Her coxswain Maynard, finding it beyond their power, determined to again re-enter the harbour. The drogue was thrown out and several seas were passed safely, but the boat was subsequently struck by a heavy cross sea on her quarter and capsized.

Ten of her crew were thrown into the surf, and two buried under her, being jammed under her thwart. The boat after some time righted, and the struggling crew clambered into her in an exhausted state.

It was then found that her rudder, oars etc were unshipped or broken, and that she was drifting with powerful outset back into the worst of the broken water. Some of her gear was entangled in the rudder, the drogue ropes and other small lines were then cut to prevent the boat being taken by the current around the back of the breakwater rocks, where no doubt she would have been lost and the crew drowned.

The lifeboat was then manned by three oars on one side, and two on the other, and a small oar shipped aft for steering. Some of the crew lay round the boat exhausted, it was not until entering still water that the coxswain was missed. This unhappy accident has caused a widow and ten young children to mourn the loss of one who was never yet found wanting in humanity, courage, and endurance on our rock bound coast.

As the body may not yet be found, it may be well to state for the sake of identification the letters "JM" are tattooed on the left arm... WDM March 1877

So it was that Thomas Ellis of Hayle, and Maynard the coxswain of the Bude lifeboat left a total of fifteen children fatherless; and there would have been only family aid, and maybe the results of a subscription fund to help support them, otherwise the choice was the workhouse. The idea of state care and responsibility was many years in the future.

This comes across very clearly in a letter from a widow to the editor of the Western Daily Mercury. She had been angered by comments from a clergyman. (A 'middie' was a midshipman.)

> Sir,
>
> I read in last Saturday's paper a letter from a Rev gentleman concerning the poor washerwomen of Plymouth. He dwells on the enormous charge which poor cadets and 'middies' have to pay for their washing. I suppose the Rev gentleman does not know the enormous charge the washerwomen of Plymouth have to pay the watermen to take them down to Plymouth Sound, or the weather the poor washerwomen have to endure in bringing home the clothes. The washerwomen do not get their money quite so easy as the Rev gentlemen does, when he is making up sermons in his study, or if he is not up to the exertion, buying them at two pence a dozen. I am a poor widow with a very large family and I remain,
>
> "A very poor washerwoman."

Modern technology has advanced so rapidly that these years of the 1870's seem now to be an eternity away. They are not of course, for there are many people alive today whose grandparents, and indeed parents would well remember this sort of grinding poverty.

They might remember other things with pride though - such as the press reports of the British clipper *Thermopylae* leaving Gravesend on the 7th November 1868, making her number with the Lizard at 6 p.m the next night, and then only sixty days later signalling for her pilot off Melbourne.

The Whitbread 'Round the World Race' is probably the toughest of today's sailboat races. I wonder if the competitors recall reading accounts of the *Ariel* and the *Taeping* racing each other home from China?

They cleared Foochow on the same tide with the new season's tea. Ninety-eight days and 14,000 miles later they were still in sight of each other as they raced into the chops of the Channel, past the Lizard and Start Point. It was *Taeping* who got her ropes ashore at London Dock twenty minutes before her rival, and they agreed to split the prize money.

Nevertheless by most standards, it was a hard way to eke out a living, and at their best, the jobs of anyone connected with the sea were often ones of sheer grinding discomfort.

Indeed I am reminded of that sermon used in St Andrews, the mother church of Plymouth, for the victims of that Titanic disaster in 1912 .

The text was from Jeremiah: "Harmath is confounded, and Arpad; for they have heard evil tidings they are fainthearted there is sorrow on the sea; it cannot be quiet."

It seems an appropriate ending, for the sea is rarely quiet, and the lives of those who were connected with it were, as we have seen, often eventful ones.

Garlandstone lies quietly in her last berth far up the River Tamar at the restored Victorian port of Morwelham.

INDEX

Abandoned vessels	45
Abramson, Capt	107
Amaland Light	75
Antiscorbutic	134
Ardrossan	73
Arweak Coastguard station	77
Assault	33
Axe, George	109, 110
Banclovich, Capt	84
Bate, Capt	87
Bates, Mr. M.P.	135
Bay of Biscay	137
Beef putrid	136
Berbet, H.	30
Bethel, Capt	53
Billingsgate	98
Blackler, Chief Officer	124
Blake, Robert	95
Board of Trade Surveyor	142
Bombay	136
Boscastle	86
Bourne, Capt John	109
Boyle, Mr	20
Breeches buoy	119
Bridgewater	80
Bristol Channel	80, 110
Brittany	73
Brixham	93, 97, 143
Brixham fishermen	96
Bude	85, 153

Bullying, belaying pins		34
"	bruising	34, 36
"	Capt and mate	34
"	shifting coal	37
"	caning	38
"	on French smack	30
"	iron bolts	34
"	kicking	35, 109
"	man overboard	29, 39
"	mastheading	39
"	Nova Scotians	33, 34
"	ropes-ending	35, 36, 39
"	scrubbing	41
"	tarring	38, 40
Burman, Capt William		87
Cadiz		107
Cane, James		97
Capsize		59
Cargoes, china clay		74
"	coal	80, 84, 111
"	rape seed	136
"	salt	107
"	salted cod	87
"	sugar	52
Carr, Alfred		137
Carstulovich, Giovanni		71
Certifcate of competency		106, 107
Chepstow		127
Chester, Capt		118
Clark, Capt		107
Clevedon		80

Clovelly	87
Collision	44
" causes	44
Congreve, Sir William	119
Cook, Capt	115
Cooper, Charles Astley	35-41
Copley medal	134
Cork lifebelts	91
Coseman, Charles	58, 59
Cox, George and John	86
Coye, Capt	107
Cress	134
Crowthers, Coxswain	127
Cutting	20
Dalmil, Capt	142
Dan, Capt	148
Davey, Owen Capt	45, 46
Davis, Capt	60
Desertion	115, 116
Dismasting	48, 50
Distress signal	51
Dodd, Capt	49-51
Dogs, trained	94
Doom Bar	126
Dried fish	87
Drift fishermen	99
Drink	107, 108
Drogue	58, 153
Drowning	94
Dufruit, Capt	54
Dyer, Richard Capt	110
Dynamite fishing	100

East Charlestown	55
East Countrymen	42
Eddy, Andrew	92, 93
Eddystone	18
" lighthouse	18
" reef	19
Ellis, John	100
Ellis, Thomas	150
Ermington, Capt Richard	144
Evans Linton	33
Evans, William	114
Falmouth	114, 138, 140
Falmouth outfitters boat	45, 46
Farland, Dennis	31, 32
Fatigue	110
Fish auction	98
Fish buyers	98
Fisher Edward	89, 90
Fishing nets	96, 102
Fish, poor quality	98
Flat, J.H	58
Flare up light	46
Fog	77
Foochow	155
Fothering	53
Fowey	115, 146
Frostbite	75
Galveston	137
Gary, Capt	58
Glasson, Thomas	129

Gorregan reef	70	Jettisoning cargo	114
Gould, Boatswain	121, 122	Johns, Richard	56, 57
Granite coast	70	Jones, Ernest	137
Greenland fisheries	143	Jones, Capt Henry	71
Gregan rocks	71	Jones, Capt John	137
Grog ships	107	Jones, Pengelly	87
Guard, Capt	86		
Guernsey	31	Kemp, Harry	28
Gun boat	99	Kergulant, Capt	119
		Kite, Capt	65
Hallsands	93, 94		
Hand Deeps	19	Land's End	20
Harp Cove	85	Lewis, Capt	140
Harries, Joseph	147	Lifeboat	
Hartland Point	88	" Albert Edward	127, 128
Hayle	57	" Elizabeth Moore	152
Hell Bay	83	" Richard Lewis	120
Herring fishermen	92	Lighthouses:	
Hicks, William	72	Bishop Rock in gale	21
Hobbler	56	Schiller wreck	25
Hogsheads	96	Eddystone	19
Honnyman, John	66	Hanoise	74
'Hot bunking'	144	Longships	20, 22, 24, 81
Hurricane	68, 82	Telegraphic apparatus	25
		Lighthouse keepers:	
Icing	75	Boyle	20
Inch, William	95	Cutting,	20
Injuries	147	Steer,	20
Italians	127	Lightships:	
Italy	127	Royal Sovereign	29
		Sevenstones	23
Jersey	74	Limejuice	134-137

Luigi Ceschi	147	Neilson, Capt	135
Lind James	134	Neilson, Capt Hans	140
Lizard	54, 145, 150	Newfoundland	87
Load lines	66	Norris, Capt	81
London	47	Nova Scotia	33
Longstones reef	110	Nova Scotian ships	33
Looe	115	Nudson, Capt	62
Lundy Island	82, 111		
		Olsen, Capt	63
Mackerel	94	O'Neil, Capt	32
Manacles	76, 77	Orange	134
Man overboard	68, 146	Osborne, Capt	132
Manure	138		
Masthead light	46	Paddon Mr	101
Masts, broken	48, 50	Padstow	125-127
Mathews Mr	105	Paraffin	137
Maynard Coxswain	153	Pascoe, Mr	104
Mayon Jean	30, 31	Patterson, Croydon	119
MaCauley Eliza	30, 31	Penarth Roads	130
McColl, Capt Robert	74	Penbarth	78
Mercantile Shipping Act	66, 137	Pengelly, William	87
Meteorological service	146	Penryn	74
Mevagissey	102	Peters, Capt	77
Mitchell, Joseph	147	Picklecombe Point	89
Mitchell, Uncle Billy	48	Pilchards	94, 95
Morgan, Oliver	129	Pilot boats	140
Mounts Bay	120	Pilot cutter	131
Mounts Bay fishery	98	Pitch	66
Mousehole	92	Pitwood, Charles	101
Mundic	130	Plimsoll, Samuel	65
Murder	118	Plymouth	92, 69, 116
Murray, James	34	Plymouth Breakwater	51
Mutiny	114		

Poor food	135	Salcombe	132
Porthleven	48, 104	Sailors' Homes	141, 147
Porthleven lifeboat	123	Sauerkraut	134
Port Isaac	94	Scanell, James	101
Portland Bill	123, 125	Scilly Isles	25, 70, 110
Portmadoc	87	Scilly Isles mob violence	41
Portugal	110	" pilots	26
Potatoes	113	" pilot gigs	26
Prawle	124	Scurvy	36, 134
Proudfoot, Richard	34	Seine net	95
Pumps	33	Sennen Cove	24, 100
Pumping	61, 81	Sevenstones Lightship	112
Putt, Capt William	132	Sevenstones Reef	110, 111
Pyrites	129	Shannon, Capt	125
		Ships' boats	131
Retarrier Ledges	24	Ships' names:	
Rigging	50	Abercaren - barque	139
Riot Act	42	*Acorn - sloop*	51-53
River Parret	80	*Albatross - schooner*	60, 61
RNLI	91	*Alexander d'Auray*	78
RNLI report	152	*Almera - fishing boat*	90
Roberts, Capt	146	*Amazon - steam tug*	126-129
Rocket apparatus	120-124	*Amiable - schooner*	130
" brigade	123	*Anna - brigantine*	62, 64
Rofoke Faita	35-39	*Anna Louisa - ketch*	127
Rogers, Capt Thomas	150	*Antelope - pilot boat*	45
Roscoff	79	*Arab - steam tug*	50
Roulle, Capt	113	*Archibald Fellar*	65
Royal Masthead	39	*Archibelle*	147
Rule of the Road	44	*Aretura - fishing boat*	48
Runners	136	*Ariel*	155
		Band of Hope - fishing boat	100

Bessie - schooner	150	*Jefferson Borton - schooner*	118
Catherine - fishing boat	104	*John and Sarah - smack*	90
Catherine Griffith	70, 71	*Julia Daniel - brigantine*	45
Ceres	76	*Lady Wodehouse - steamer*	29
Colibri - brig	138	*Leader - schooner*	148, 149
Dorotea - schooner	58, 59	*Lilly - brig*	31
Ely - paddle-steamer	81	*Lion - gig*	81
Estelle - schooner	58, 59	*Lochan - fishing sloop*	94, 95
Ethel - brigantine	47, 48	*Lord Bute - steamboat*	85
Ethel - schooner	110	*Loretta - barquentine*	61
Exhibition - smack	74	*Maggie Dixon - barque*	34
Esmerelda - sloop	45, 46	*Marco Primogenito - barque*	84
Fanny - ketch	80	*Maria - smack*	86
Fanny - schooner	108	*Marie Francois - sloop*	113
Fortune	147	*Mary Ann Storey - lifeboat*	76
Freja	140	*Membry - fishing boat*	89
Gallant - schooner	81	*Merry Lass - fishing boat*	147
Garfield - barque	137	*Message - schooner*	131
Gelart - steamboat	64	*Millie Bain*	115
Glen Monarch	32	*Mohegan - passenger liner*	76
Gloucester - whaleboat	65	*Naide - schooner*	77
Goethe - barque	47, 48	*Nebraska - fishing boat*	96
Hawke - barque	144	*Nellie - fishing boat*	148
Idris - schooner	88	*New Parliament - schooner*	
Ilva - barque	107		82, 83, 85
Immaculate - brigantine	127	*Orient - brigantine*	116
Integrity	25, 27	*Penar - schooner*	57
Jaques Cartier - brig	74	*Physician - schooner*	51-53
Jaques Marie - sloop	53, 54	*Ponthien - brig*	123
Jane Avery - barque	49-51	*Queen of the Bay - tug*	43
Jane Stewart - schooner	114	*Rippling Wave*	146
Jeanne - pilot cutter	74	*River Lune - barque*	73

Robert Young - sloop	92
Rose of Torridge	86, 87
Sandberg - barque	131
Sarpaborg - brig	63
Secret - fishing boat	118
S.S.Schiller - liner	24
St.David - steamboat	80
Stouer - fishing boat	74
Strasbourg - barque	147
Sunbeam	142
Taeping	155
The Daylight	107
The Janet	56
The Norman	46
Thermopylae - clipper	154
S.S Titantic	155
Topaz - brigantine	66, 67
Truelove - barque	143
Union - smack	30
Utility - schooner	125
Victory - punt	87
Victoria - tug	81, 82
Wave of Clovelly - skiff	87
WLJ - barque	109
Sidelights	137
Singlehanded	64, 65
Sleep, William	95
Smeaton's Tower	18
Soper Mr	101
Spain	110
St. Agnes	25, 27, 72

St. Agnes Lighthouse	70, 71
Start Point	123, 125
Starvation	59, 136
St. Aubyn, Sir John	120
'Staying'	123
Steer	20
Stepper Point	83
St. Ives	95
St. Mary's	27
St. Minver	83
Subscription fund	101, 105
Suffocation	148
Swansea	45
Taylor, Walter	145
Teignmouth	103
Tonkins, Edgar	92
Topsails	128
Torcross	129
Tranmore Bay	108
Trawls	45, 46
Tregier	74
Trewhella, Coxswain	120
Trinity House	22
Trinity Pilots	85
Troytown	72
Tucker, Samuel	98
Tusker	84
Unseaworthy ships	142, 143
Union company	95

Vermin   148
Vinegar   36
Vivian, George   108

Warning lights   46, 124
Waterford harbour   108
Watchkeeping   46, 49, 137
Watts, William   66
'Wearing',   123
Weather forecasting   146
West, Capt   73
Western Islands   139
Westhook buoy   81
Whale   102, 103
Whaleboat   65
Wheatstone, Capt Robert   127
Wine   87
Wolf Rock lighthouse   21
Workhouse,   154
Wreckage   84